Fields of Green

The Simpler Way to Wealth

TERRY BROWN

iUniverse, Inc.
Bloomington

Fields of Green
The Simpler Way to Wealth

Copyright © 2012 by Terry Brown

All rights reserved. No part of this book may be used or reproduced by any means, graphic, electronic, or mechanical, including photocopying, recording, taping or by any information storage retrieval system without the written permission of the publisher except in the case of brief quotations embodied in critical articles and reviews.

The information, ideas, and suggestions in this book are not intended to render professional advice. Before following any suggestions contained in this book, you should consult your personal accountant or other financial advisor. Neither the author nor the publisher shall be liable or responsible for any loss or damage allegedly arising as a consequence of your use or application of any information or suggestions in this book.

iUniverse books may be ordered through booksellers or by contacting:

iUniverse
1663 Liberty Drive
Bloomington, IN 47403
www.iuniverse.com
1-800-Authors (1-800-288-4677)

Because of the dynamic nature of the Internet, any web addresses or links contained in this book may have changed since publication and may no longer be valid. The views expressed in this work are solely those of the author and do not necessarily reflect the views of the publisher, and the publisher hereby disclaims any responsibility for them.

Any people depicted in stock imagery provided by Thinkstock are models, and such images are being used for illustrative purposes only.

Certain stock imagery © Thinkstock.

ISBN: 978-1-4759-5458-6 (sc)
ISBN: 978-1-4759-5460-9 (hc)
ISBN: 978-1-4759-5459-3 (e)

Printed in the United States of America

iUniverse rev. date: 11/02/2012

Dedication

IN MY VOYAGE OF writing a book for the first time, I would like to first and foremost thank my lovely wife of twenty-five years, Stephanie, who supported me wholeheartedly in my efforts. She is the author in our family, so I wish to thank her for her guidance and encouragement. Without her, this book would not have been possible.

Also, I wish to thank my children, Savannah and Cameron, for encouraging me and allowing me to selfishly spend some of their time for my personal efforts. I hope some day they might be able to find what's in the book to be of help in living within this challenging financial world.

In addition, I wish to thank my parents, Earl and Susie Brown, for their guidance and examples in living the truly good life. Without a doubt, they provided me the framework to be successful. I would also like to thank my brother, Craig, for always being there and showing me the true example of perseverance.

I would like to thank my mother-in-law, Rita Ray, for showing me firsthand how a single mom can, through hard work and dedication, raise three children and provide them all with a college education in this great country of ours.

Lastly, I would like to thank my great uncle James, who at the tender age of ninety-three still gets up every morning to check how many eggs his hens will allow him to sell for the day. I think of him often and how he has remained true to his values all these many years.

Contents

Dedication	v
Preface	ix
1. Needs: Give Abraham His Due	1
2. Wants: Do You Really Want That?	5
3. Net Worth: So Where Am I?	11
4. Assets: What We Own	19
5. Liabilities: What We Owe	27
6. Hang with Me	37
7. Investments and Insurance	39
8. Insurance: Term or Whole?	49
9. College Funding	55
10. Tax Avoidance: Don't Get Carried Away	63
11. 'Tis Better to Receive—Part 1	71
12. 'Tis Better to Receive …Cash!—Part 2	77
13. What We Live In	83
14. Money on Wheels	91

15. How to Earn a 17.5 Percent Return 105
16. Don't Fall in Love with These Two Things 117
17. It Bears Repeating—Part 1. 123
18. It Bears Repeating—Part 2. 127
19. Texting behind Home Plate 131
20. I Think I'm Done. 137

Preface

As a novice writer, beginning a book from scratch is similar to a bashful five-year-old walking into my wife's kindergarten room on the first day of school. You don't know where to start and which direction to go, but you know you must do something. That is how I feel as I approach the task of putting into words what I have been thinking for the past several years.

Unfortunately, for the majority of diehard readers, what I have been thinking doesn't sell in terms of romance or intrigue. Rather, my thoughts come from a focus on finance and practicality and from my belief that we Americans in particular need to change the way we make financial decisions.

In my early adult years, I toyed with the idea of becoming a college accounting instructor, from my desire to help people. Though my eventual course of actions never took me down that career path, I nonetheless formed a mental framework as to what type of teacher I would have been.

Two things come to mind. One is credibility. Has my teacher ever engaged himself in the subject he or she is teaching? If so, credibility is definitely enhanced. The second is simplicity. No matter how complex some of us like to think our jobs are, everything can be reduced to the basic elements. The greatest teachers realize their true value is in reducing the complicated into simple concepts that build over time in the classroom.

Fall of 2008 is a time that I look back upon and see the trigger for my desire to write a book. For the first time in my adult life, I witnessed metal, energy, and grain prices go through the roof in just a few months. I also saw the financial pain upon many Americans as real estate collapsed and workers lost jobs. I distinctly recall gasoline being $4.00 a gallon in October, only to fall to $1.50 by the end of the year. It was truly a scary time for many.

It was also a time when I began to think, "Why not me?" as I occasionally walked through a bookstore, wondering whether I could write something of a financial nature. More importantly, my thoughts progressed to questioning if I truly had something to offer. In my opinion, there is nothing worse than listening to someone who overvalues the worth of his or her message. You will indeed find that to be a real concern if you consider writing a book, especially if you place a premium upon humility.

So now I suppose you are thinking, "Why you?" Why read something written by a midforties accountant from rural western Kentucky? Two things come to mind. One is credibility, and the second is simplicity. From a humble perspective, my feeling of credibility comes from nearly twenty-five years of financial experience in general, and individual tax preparation in particular. Thanks to my clients, I have been given a wealth of financial observations from which to draw upon and share. For that insight, I freely admit I have received more than I have given.

As far as simplicity is concerned, putting seed into Mother Earth's good soil taught me so much growing up on the farm. If you've never been there, you truly don't know what you have missed. And if you have experienced it, as I have, you don't quite realize the full value of your experiences until later in life.

The title of the book, *Fields of Green: The Simpler Way to Wealth*, was chosen as the best description of how I view myself and my way of thinking. The farm life gave me a very strong basis for simplicity, logic, and blind faith. There is nothing simpler than dirt, yet it is so simple that most of us overlook its raw power.

I believe the same can be said for human achievement. Just like dirt mixed with a seed of corn, our abilities in their simplest form have so much potential when presented with the right opportunities. Contrary to what Wall Street would have us to believe, one doesn't need to be an Ivy League graduate to attain personal wealth. To be blunt, if I can do it, then anyone can.

On a personal level, I have been able to accumulate more wealth than I ever thought possible through a healthy dose of common sense principles, many of them realized before I became an adult. Education can be a tremendous means to unlock one's potential, yet I feel we too often cheat ourselves from the merits of discipline, simplicity, and common sense.

To that end, my goal in this book is to challenge you to rethink financial stereotypes and reduce the seemingly complex to simple practicality. The first six chapters are designed to assess where you are financially and to ask why you do things from a financial perspective. The remaining chapters are devoted to specific topics and advice that I believe are critical in coping within today's challenging financial environment.

Similar to the "less is more" analogy, simplicity is the key to better understanding and knowledge. I sincerely hope you find that to be the case as you read these words by a common farm boy from Kentucky.

Chapter 1

Needs: Give Abraham His Due

In both high school and college I never had a problem studying things I liked, especially math and business. However, I would not have given a dime to take another psychology or sociology course. For some reason, those just never captured my interest. However, in psychology I managed to retain two pieces of knowledge. One was B. F. Skinner and his tests with rats. The other was Abraham Maslow and the hierarchy of needs.

Basically, Maslow's hierarchy categorized needs from the most critical at the base of the triangle, upward to the less critical needs at the top. Examples of most critical needs are food, clothing, and shelter, while lower priority needs would be self-esteem and social approval.

Perhaps because I am a simple thinker, Maslow's hierarchy appealed to me. It just made sense that until you satisfied the basic needs of food, clothing, and shelter, all else didn't really matter.

In my grandparents' generation, and to a slightly lesser extent in my parents' generation, the base of Mr. Maslow's hierarchy pretty much summed up life in my part of the world. If you were clothed, fed, and had a nice home, you had the good life.

However, in my generation, particularly in the 1980s, advances in technology took a strong hold, and the advances have since accelerated at a dizzying pace. Specifically, a household's "basic need" of phone service as defined thirty years ago has changed drastically by today's standards. As a teenager, I distinctly remember having a four-party house phone, which we had to share with three elderly ladies down the road. Try carrying on a teen social life with that kind of communication network today. Now, the term "basic need" would encompass a private land line, two or three cell phones, texting, and Internet service.

Generations ago, education through high school was considered a great asset, and college was looked upon as almost an elite privilege. Today, high school education has become a bare necessity, and a college education has become more of a need than a luxury.

In both examples, advancements have naturally come at a cost. In many cases, per-unit consumer costs have actually decreased, such as long-distance phone service. However, the scope of services we now have at our disposal has expanded so that overall household costs have increased. In simple terms, our former wants have become needs, and we have been introduced to new wants along the way. Such is the territory that comes with a higher standard of living.

Whether we care to admit it, we all have hierarchies of needs and wants. In general, I think it is safe to assume that we would share Maslow's three basic needs of food, clothing, and shelter. Beyond that, we could fill in charts of needs and wants that would be as diverse as the American population.

Are three cars in a household a need or a want? Is an inground pool a need or a want? The truth of the matter is there is no right or wrong answer. Rather, I think it is merely a good exercise to assess one's definition of needs and wants, as this is undoubtedly something that we as a society rarely stop to consider. Hopefully, this will come back to you as a frame of reference as you read later chapters.

According to how you define your needs, the related costs are essentially what it is going to take for you to exist in terms of financial responsibilities. I prefer to label these as *fixed costs*, because as long as your heart keeps beating, the financial commitment must be made. This concept would apply to food, in particular. The need is always there, or fixed.

If you care to know my modern-day version of Maslow's needs, I would list in order of importance as follows: (1) food, clothing, and shelter (2) a vehicle and fuel to drive to work (3) insurance and health care, and (4) college education for my children. Granted, there are other things I could put on this list. But in keeping things simple, these four categories pretty much describe what drives me to get out of bed on cold winter mornings and go to work.

Simply put, I am driven from within to meet my definition of needs. Otherwise, I fail my family and possibly my very existence.

Summary Points
- ***Yesterday's wants have become today's needs.***
- ***A more advanced society means more cost commitments.***
- ***Maslow's hierarchy of needs helps explain how we spend our money.***

Chapter 1 Exercise

List the top five needs, in order of priority, that drive you to be a financial provider. Then estimate the annual costs of these needs.

Need	**Annual cost**
1._____	1._____
2._____	2._____
3._____	3._____
4._____	4._____
5._____	5._____

TOTAL_____

Chapter 2

Wants: Do You Really Want That?

I AM A FIRM believer in the 80/20 principle, which can be applied to a great many facets of life. For instance, I have often heard it stated that in a group setting, whether charitable or business, 20 percent of the people do 80 percent of the work. While I do not hold this to be an absolute truth, I do think the concept has a good bit of validity.

In presenting my thoughts, I likewise feel there is an 80/20 ratio of relevance to the population of potential readers. For example, on the upper extreme of income levels, there is a group of people who will manage to spend every dime they possess. Individuals who immediately come to mind are professional athletes with multimillion-dollar contracts. I realize it is the overall exception, but in my opinion we hear way too many instances of these individuals in bankruptcy. Personally, I just cannot fathom how one can spend that much money, but this indeed happens. Within this group, I don't think I have much range of relevance to help.

On the flip side, I know more than a few individuals who have raised children alone on a modest income, in many cases providing the children with good college educations. Other individuals who come to mind have done the same after facing extreme medical hardships and related costs. I absolutely commend these individuals and maintain that they should be writing their own books.

As for the remaining 80 percent, this is the group to whom I hope to be relevant, and to whom I can most readily identify. For instance, like most people, I do not share the opinion of some conservative financial experts who maintain that one should not aspire to own a home. These folks believe it is better to rent for one's entire life due to the long-term costs associated with home ownership.

My quick answer to this thinking is, yes, if we think we should live our personal lives as a business, then renting may be the better option. But I'm a firm believer in the American dream, and believe that we all should live where we truly want to live and within our means in the type of home that makes us happy.

Another thing that comes to mind is I do not agree with those who insist that everything should be purchased free of debt. Simply put, if you don't have all the cash, then don't buy the goods. Though I understand the basis of the reasoning, I like to think of myself as a practical person. Sometimes life doesn't give us all the opportunities to buy everything in cash.

Now let's go back to the theme of wants as they apply within the 80 percent group. Foremost, we know our financial commitments to *needs* cannot be avoided. But likewise, the financial costs of our *wants* cannot be avoided either. To me, this is the centerpiece of the financial problems in our country.

As consumers, we are continually bombarded with advertisements to buy everything under the sun as we watch sporting events, drive down the highway, explore the Internet, or even stand at the urinal in a restaurant. Throw in the convenience of a credit card and the "click and sold" features of the Internet, and you have all the ingredients for extreme challenges to even the most financially disciplined individuals.

Having said all of that, here is another mental exercise. Broadly speaking, identify your set of wants, given your current economic situation, or what I would call your financial reality. For me, it would be these major categories: (1) more than one vehicle (for convenience), (2) a home with a big yard and pool, (3) ability to take multiple vacations each year, and (4) being able to provide our children with a few of the nicer things in life.

Going a step further, is there anything on your list that you question whether you truly want it? Of the items I have listed, there isn't anything to which I only have a lukewarm feeling. However, if I were asked to double the list, perhaps I would start to question my genuine desire for one or more of the additional items. It goes back to the principle of utility I learned years ago in a basic economics class. The first cheeseburger tastes mighty good when you're hungry, but the second and third just don't have the same positive effect.

PERSONAL REFLECTION
Have you ever done anything expensive that you really didn't want to do? I am of the opinion that many families overextend themselves on vacations merely because of peer pressure, especially social circles within our schools. Along similar lines, how many families cave in to the pressure from a son or daughter to get an expensive first car? I have seen this a great deal over the past decade, in particular, and I am convinced that certain parents become too absorbed in the hype of keeping up with what other parents down the street purchase for their children.

Don't get me wrong. I strongly believe in spending money for the good things in life. I do this personally in the form of weekend getaways, sporting events, and vacations on the beach. As for expensive colognes, personal jewelry, or having to drive the most recent model of car, these don't do much for me, so, therefore, my money doesn't go there. However, if I did choose to spend money on these items without a genuine desire to do so, this would be the flaw in my own financial house in that I would be spending money for the wrong reason.

Wants are fine to have, but we need to stop and question what truly drives us to have these things. Is it for happiness, or the appearance of happiness? That is somewhat deep, but I truly believe this is a real issue today. In my opinion, we have become a society too much occupied with who we are, what brand we are wearing, where we are going, and with whom we are seen.

In short, today's higher standard of living has brought with it more financial complexities to numerous households. Needs must be met, as well as our wants. So far, we have only stopped to question whether there is anything we currently possess that we truly do not need, or perhaps do not want. Some common things that come to mind are unused gym memberships, extra television packages, a boat, RV, vacation home, or a timeshare. In some instances, these are items that can accumulate to a substantial amount of money.

All I would ask of any person would be to consider why one would spend money on something for the wrong reason. That has been the sole focus of the first two chapters. If you come up with an item or two that you can eliminate, then the time so far will have been well justified. Much of the remainder of the book will now focus on how best to manage the costs of those things we have identified that we need and that we truly want.

Summary Points
- *Wants are good and can be strong motivators in giving us fulfilling lives.*
- *The danger of wants is often pursuing them for the wrong reasons.*
- *Excess wants and lack of financial discipline are serious issues today.*

Chapter 2 Exercise

List your top five wants in order of importance to you, as well as the estimated annual costs. This can be a wish list as well as items that you currently possess.

<u>Want</u> **<u>Annual cost</u>**

1._____ 1._____
2._____ 2._____
3._____ 3._____
4._____ 4._____
5._____ 5._____

TOTAL_____

Now write the primary reason for wishing to attain each of your wants listed above.

1._____
2._____
3._____
4._____
5._____

CHAPTER 3

Net Worth: So Where Am I?

HAVE YOU EVER FOUND yourself alone in a strange mall for the first time? After a few minutes, you end up in a place you don't recognize. It is almost as if you are on a ship at sea without a compass, especially if you happen to be of the male persuasion. But if you are lucky enough to find a map, you can, fortunately, right your path if you first locate where you are in the mall. It will do no good to take off blindly until you first identify your current position and then plan your route accordingly.

Such is the goal after we have gone through the first two chapters, considering those things that we need and want in life. It does no good to question our spending habits if we do not follow through with an analysis of where we are in financial terms, or again, our financial reality.

How often have you heard the comment, "There's no telling what he is worth"? Have you ever stopped and questioned what the term "worth" truly means? So many times American society in general looks at the glitter of a person and draws a conclusion based on that factor alone. Conversely, we are guilty just the same of looking at one's lack of glitter and concluding in the opposite direction.

Suffice it to say that I've seen individuals with the finest of everything who couldn't afford to pay their next bill, and I've seen individuals who lived like a pauper who had the means to purchase an entire bank. We must realize it's not so much *what we have* that determines our worth, but *how much we owe.* There is a huge difference.

Before I move on, I will readily admit the following exercise isn't something I have diligently followed during my adult years. Rather, it has been more of a thought process that I would casually put on a piece of paper every now and then. It seems in the first years of one's career, one focuses mainly on the earnings from his or her job and the items that need to be purchased. And in defense of that mentality, many Americans enter their working careers with not a great deal of net worth. Thus, here is a concept that doesn't seem to generate much attention until a person is perhaps well in his or her thirties.

Quite simply, net worth is the value of all assets owned, less any debts owed. If one is married, the calculation would thus include all assets and obligations of the spouse as well. In keeping the topic simple, here is a suggested summary of the calculation.

Assets

Cash in banks, cash on hand   _____

+ Certificates of deposit   _____

+ Value of owned automobiles   _____

+ Value of owned residence   _____

+ Value of stocks, bonds (outside of retirement plan)   _____

+ Value of 401(k), pension plans, IRAs   _____

+ Value of land, vacation homes   _____

+ Value of owned business (net worth)   _____

+ Other   _____

                    Total Assets   _____

Liabilities

Credit card balances owed   _____

\+ Debt on automobiles   _____

\+ Debt on residence   _____

\+ Debt on land, vacation homes   _____

\+ Debt against 401(k) balances   _____

\+ Other   _____

                                      Total Liabilities   _____

       NET WORTH = *Total Assets less*   _____
                               Total Liabilities

To make the above calculation any more complicated is in my opinion a useless waste of time. This is a simple exercise that requires only two things: (1) a small amount of time, and (2) a decision of how often to measure your net worth. The calculation can be done quarterly, as 401(k) and pension information is generally updated this frequently. Otherwise, a semiannual or even an annual calculation will suffice. The key is to simply sit down and take the time to do the calculation. Many will be surprised in both directions.

Granted, some of the asset valuations may be somewhat subjective, such as the value of a personal residence or the current value of one's pension. In these cases I recommend erring on the low side. Following this approach will ensure your net worth calculation to be more conservatively realistic.

From a mathematical standpoint one can easily see from the net worth equation why so many Americans ended up in financial distress after the real estate collapse in 2008. More specifically, those individuals with expensive personal residences and vacation homes that were highly leveraged with debt were affected as the values of the assets plunged, while the underlying debt obligations stayed the same. Hence, net worth took a direct hit.

Such is the risk of relying too much on debt when one assumes asset values will forever keep escalating. We can't have it both ways. When asset values climb and the related debt stays constant, we are thrilled. But when asset values plummet, how can we not expect the result to be different? We simply cannot have our cake, and eat it too.

From a diagnostic standpoint, I won't pretend to have some magic scale of measurement as to where one should be in terms of net worth. So many factors play into the assessment, such as age, number of children, college expenses, volatility of the assets (such as stocks), and financial lifestyle of the individual. Attempting to come up with some kind of a scorecard for net worth would at best be a stab in the dark that might be relevant to only a small percentage. Rather, I prefer to use the net worth calculation as a means to establish a self-analysis starting point to help achieve better financial discipline down the road.

A former coworker of mine who was in charge of energy usage analysis for our aluminum plant often made a statement that left an impression on me. His signature statement was, "If it can't be measured, it's not worth doing." Why go through the exercise of saving energy if you don't first take the time to see where you currently stand?

Such is the case in making the initial determination of net worth. From there, you don't need to worry about how you are doing versus others. All you need to worry about is relating your current net worth to where you started in order to determine if you are headed in the right direction.

So before moving on, here are two basic statements I will make on the topic of net worth:

1. If you're in the negative, that is obviously not good. Technically, you are considered to be *insolvent*. In this case, one needs to focus on decreasing debts, starting with those on which you are paying the highest rate of interest. Additionally, it is imperative that some degree of savings be accomplished in order to positively impact net worth, no matter how small the savings might be. Otherwise, continued spending in excess of income will only deepen the negative net worth position.

2. If you are on the positive side of the calculation, that is great. But just how positive are you? Ideally, the older you are the higher the net worth should be. Again, the concept is so simple. The difficulty is exercising the financial discipline to focus on saving while maintaining a modest approach to spending.

In summary, we have now devoted the first two chapters to questioning our needs and wants, and the third chapter to measuring our financial health. The former chapters pertain more to our *financial behavior*, while the latter looks more to our current *financial condition*. To use a physical analogy, the first chapters relate to what we eat and our diet habits, while the third chapter lets us know how much we weigh at the starting point.

I know it sounds overly basic, but I challenge you to question yourself as to whether you have ever taken the time to calculate something as simple as your net worth. If not, why would anything more complicated be of any value in our attempt to improve financially? I would compare it to my trying to understand the latest advancement in open heart surgery in dealing with a recurring chest pain. Simplicity definitely has a place and is too often ignored in our quest for more sophisticated answers.

Summary Points
- *Wealth is measured not only by assets, but by liabilities as well.*
- *One should assess one's net worth at least twice a year.*
- *Large incomes do not guarantee sufficient net worth at retirement.*

CHAPTER 3 EXERCISE

Calculate your current personal net worth in the first column. Then, later update the numbers in the second column (after three months) to measure the change.

	Measurement Date #1 ___/___/___	Measurement Date #2 ___/___/___
Assets		
Cash in banks, cash on hand	_____	_____
+ Certificates of deposit	_____	_____
+ Value of owned automobiles	_____	_____
+ Value of owned residence	_____	_____
+ Value of stocks, bonds (outside of retirement plan)	_____	_____
+ Value of 401(k), pension plans, IRAs	_____	_____
+ Value of land, vacation homes	_____	_____
+ Value of owned business (net worth)	_____	_____
+ Other	_____	_____
Total Assets	_____	_____

	Measurement Date #1 ___/___/___	Measurement Date #2 ___/___/___
Liabilities		
Credit card balances owed	_____	_____
+ Debt on automobiles	_____	_____
+ Debt on residence	_____	_____
+ Debt on land, vacation homes	_____	_____
+ Debt against 401(k) balances	_____	_____
+ Other	_____	_____
Total Liabilities	_____	_____
NET WORTH = *Total Assets less Total Liabilities*	_____	_____

As a follow-up to your calculation, identify the items that are impacting your net worth the most positively and negatively. Is there anything you can do to enhance the positives and reduce the negatives? If so, the end result will be contributions to net worth.

Most positive: _____

Most negative: _____

Fields of Green

CHAPTER 4

Assets: What We Own

FROM OUR DISCUSSION OF net worth, we can easily see that such value can be increased by either increasing our assets (things owned), or decreasing our liabilities (things owed). But in reality, it is very difficult to separate the two. This chapter focuses on the asset side of the net worth equation.

ONE LIVING THE DREAM LIFE
The accumulation of quantities and types of assets has a large correlation to Maslow's hierarchy of needs. By way of illustration, let us use some imagination, and assume you move to another country to start a career fresh out of college. Because you have agreed to move to a remote location, your salary is very substantial. However, once you step off the plane, you really have nothing to your name other than the cash in your wallet.

So what are the first items to be bought? More than likely, food and a place to live will be the first expenditures. After that, perhaps you will need new clothing to adapt to your new climate. As weeks progress, you may begin to look for a house to own rather than a rental apartment. Or perhaps an automobile will take priority, depending upon the distance to your new job and the local transportation choices.

In reality, each of our individual circumstances isn't a great deal different from this hypothetical example. The first dollars of any person's income must be used to attend to the higher priorities of life—our basic needs. After that, our wants become a part of the decision-making process as we contemplate whether to spend additional money or save. In most cases, there is never an issue of what to do with the money left over. As we all know, Americans do not set the financial bar when it comes to thriftiness.

Taking our example a step further, assume your new job is paying $500,000 per year, and you are single. I know this is stepping out of the bounds of reality, but sometimes a stretch from the normal way of thinking can help bring a point home much clearer. In this case, unless you just have some sort of financial sickness, you will reach a point where you will stop and question what you should do with your excess money. No doubt this would be a fine problem to have.

Let us now put a little realism into the example and assume that a salary of $500,000 will cost you $150,000 in taxes, as we know the government must get its share. This leaves $350,000 in *disposable income*, more commonly referred to as *take-home pay*. Now, I wish to divide what you could do with your money into five general categories:

Level	Category	Description	Examples
1	Maslow items	Items needed for basic survival	Food, clothing, mortgage interest, or rent
2	Modern Maslow items	Items needed in the modern world	Car to get to work, furniture
3	Toys	Pleasure assets	Sports car, RV, giant stereo system
4	Retirement investments	Plans that give one incentive to set aside money for retirement	401(k) plans, IRAs

| 5 | Nonretirement investments | Assets that generate income and/or appreciate | Stocks, bonds, land, equity in personal home, or vacation home |

Now, assuming levels 1 and 2 expenditures consume a generous $100,000 of the disposable income, you still have $250,000 left to spend on toys and investments. After spending $50,000 on a new sports car (level 3), let's assume you set aside another $50,000 at your work in various retirement investments (level 4) to plan for the future. More than likely, your employer will have some matching feature to encourage you to set aside the maximum amount of pay allowed by tax law. So even after this, you would still have $150,000 of your $500,000 salary to spend, save, or a combination of the two.

Whether we realize it or not, this is where the concept of risk inevitably enters the equation. Quite simply, safe and insured certificates of deposit generate lousy returns because the investor is protected from almost all possible risk of losing principal. Therefore, a low return on the money is the reward. On the other hand, one willing to lose much if not all of his or her investment can in some cases realize substantial returns. An example of this would be investing in stock of a small, unproven company that appears to have a product or service with the potential to thrive.

This chapter is not devoted to suggestions on how to spend the excess $150,000 in our example, as this will be discussed later. Rather, suffice to say that where an individual decides to invest any excess money will depend very much on his or her financial discipline and tolerance to risk.

I realize that presenting a hypothetical example of one living alone on a $500,000 salary might sound irrelevant. However, the point to be made is that such an individual would soon have to face decisions on where to invest that excess money. This assumption only underscores my amazement as to how some professional athletes can go through so much money and come out broke.

Referring back to our five levels of assets, a fortunate individual making $500,000 per year would under normal circumstances follow the order of levels 1 through 5 in spending his or her income. To make the point clear, it would be nearly impossible to get to the level 5 asset purchases without first having at least a decent sum of money to make such financial choices. This is where I now hope to hit home with reality.

ONE LIVING THE REAL LIFE

Let us now change the circumstances and assume another individual makes $60,000 per year in the United States, again fresh out of college. After an assumed tax of $10,000, we know that levels 1 and 2 items must be purchased in order to live and move to and from the new job.

The $50,000 of disposable income would perhaps be reduced by $35,000 for basic needs (food, clothing, and shelter) in a typical situation where the individual was somewhat frugal. The reality of the situation is this individual now has $15,000 to apply toward levels 3, 4, and 5 assets, whereas the individual in our first example had a comparable amount of $250,000.

Below is a summary of the two hypothetical cases:

	Dream life	**Real life**
Salary	$ 500,000	$ 60,000
Less income taxes	(150,000)	(10,000)
Disposable income	350,000	50,000
Less levels 1 and 2	(100,000)	(35,000)
Available for levels 3, 4, and 5	250,000	15,000

Given that our second example is fairly common in the United States, and my belief is that it truly is, I have very deep concerns over trends I have witnessed over the past twenty years. Again, we are talking about $15,000 left to purchase the following:

Level 3—Toys
Level 4—Employer retirement investments
Level 5—Nonretirement investments

A generation ago, this amount of money would have been a nice residual amount to have at one's disposal. However, today's financial environment is such that this amount represents a challenge for many individuals.

For one, employer-funded pensions have been steadily declining since the 1980s as employers have looked for ways to squeeze out profits in the face of escalating health care and other cost pressures. In the good ole days, it was not uncommon for an individual to retire with both a pension (fully funded by the employer) and a 401(k) retirement plan that included substantial matching contributions from the employer. Thus, nice retirement balances were often accumulated without a significant investment from the employees.

Second, there is no doubt that the appetite of society to buy toys has grown immensely over the past few decades. This has been discussed in prior chapters, but the reality of the fact is that during this same time span Americans have needed to have more focus on setting aside additional money for retirement investments rather than pleasure assets.

In short, more of the typical $15,000 "leftover" money in US households has been going toward the level 3 toys at the expense of funding less and less level 4 assets. In some cases, employees have reduced their 401(k) withholdings down to very low percentages, taking free money off the table in the form of reduced employer matching. In the worst cases, employees are choosing to withdraw their 401(k) balances, paying the income taxes plus the 10 percent penalty tax, and, not the least, taking away their balance upon which future earnings could be generated.

Last of all, what do you think has happened to the purchase of the level 5 assets, or nonretirement investments, during this same period? The question is somewhat rhetorical. Sadly, this type of investment has pretty much fallen off the charts for many American households. And again, this has happened during a time when employer funding for pensions has been reduced as well.

My significant concern is that someday the financial hardships now faced by so many of these individuals will pale in comparison to the difficulties they will face during their retirement years. I say that with all the sincerity that I can muster.

In summary, we have identified assets to be the positive side of the net worth equation and have categorized these assets into five areas. Levels 1 through 3 are basically needs and wants that for all practical purposes won't bring cash back to us. Level 4 assets, or retirement investments, have, in my opinion, been sacrificed in the pursuit of short-term wants. Level 5 assets, or nonretirement investments, have similarly been reduced as well, with the possible exception of personal residences. Below is a summary of the financial patterns among the five groups of assets:

Level	Category	General financial pattern
1	Maslow items	Cash goes out, rarely returns
2	Modern Maslow items	Cash goes out, rarely returns in full
3	Toys	Cash goes out, rarely returns in full
4	Retirement investments	Cash goes out, usually returns both principal plus earnings and/or appreciation
5	Nonretirement investments	Cash goes out, usually returns both principal plus earnings and/or appreciation

If you recall, levels 4 and 5 assets are the two types that in general bring your money back to you, plus earnings. So they are the good guys you want to have. Note that I have included personal residences as an investment, but I choose to put a disclaimer on that concept because the only way to realize the investment is to sell the house, and we all know we have to live somewhere. Therefore, I never quite view a personal residence as a viable investment, except perhaps in one's later years.

Admittedly, this chapter hasn't done much for you in regard to how best to invest your money in assets, but that wasn't the intention. Instead, I wished to label the variety of expenditures into five simple categories. Similar to the chapters devoted to needs and wants, I want us to pause here and evaluate what we own and why we own the things we have.

Summary Points
- *Assets explain what we purchase with our disposable income (after taxes).*
- *Levels 1, 2, and 3 assets meet our immediate needs and wants.*
- *Levels 4 and 5 assets are needed to plan for a comfortable retirement.*
- *Many Americans are seriously short in retirement funding.*

Chapter 4 Exercise

Define each of the levels of assets (or categories) that have been discussed in the chapter. For example, Level 3 would be answered as "Toys."

Level 1 _____
Level 2 _____
Level 3 _____
Level 4 _____
Level 5 _____

On a personal level, identify at least two assets that you own within each of the five levels of assets.

Level 1 _____
Level 2 _____
Level 3 _____
Level 4 _____
Level 5 _____

After identifying your assets, evaluate whether your list is well-balanced. Do you feel you have sufficient levels 4 and 5 assets to take care of future spending at retirement?

CHAPTER 5

Liabilities: What We Owe

CONTRARY TO WHAT MANY financial experts claim, the concept of liabilities, or debt, isn't necessarily a bad thing. If not for the banking system, many families would not be able to enjoy the advantages of home ownership, so vital to the US economy. From a business perspective, there have been many successful acquisitions that would never have occurred without the ability to borrow money. And from the standpoint of professions, there are many reputable doctors who owe much of their success to financial resources from student loans.

The topic of debt is in many ways tied to the concept of net worth and the five levels of assets discussed in the last chapter. In theory, it is difficult for many individuals to amass net worth and assets without some level of debt. The trick is knowing how to manage one's total debt and tracing such to the underlying assets purchased. In other words, one should always be able to explain one's debt payments.

BUYING LEVEL 1 ASSETS

Does it make any sense to borrow money at your local bank to go to the grocery and purchase food? You have an obvious answer to that question, but have you really stopped to rationalize why that is the case? The practical reasoning is it just doesn't make sense to borrow money for food. But in reality, one should never borrow money to buy something that is going to either waste away or be consumed in a week's time.

What about using debt to purchase clothing, another short-lived asset? Assuming a normal middle-class American, one should never go into debt to purchase clothing. One may purchase the clothing through the convenience of a credit card, but the debt should be paid off the next month without payment of interest. Therefore, this would not be considered debt.

As for the remaining item from Maslow's list of three basic needs, housing is somewhat of an anomaly in the level 1 classification as it pertains to debt. Housing is not quite the necessity of needing food and clothing, but it definitely ranks right up there since people need shelter to protect themselves and their possessions. However, the obvious difference with housing is the magnitude of the up-front cost in comparison to food and clothing.

Remember, in our definition of assets we label housing *interest* or *rent* as level 1 expenditures, while the *principal* portion of mortgage payments is defined as a level 5 item, or a form of long-term investment. The distinction here lies in the fact that payment of principal builds equity, while payment of interest is a cost of using someone else's money.

A typical family of four would perhaps pay $20,000 a year for food and $10,000 on clothing and personal effects. Furthermore, a new house costing $150,000 would not be out of the norm, likely requiring bank financing over twenty to thirty years.

But what about the year after the house is purchased? Again, the food and clothing would still require at least the same $30,000. Also, the house would still be there, hopefully not needing to be replaced. Ideally, one would expect the house to serve such a function for at least thirty years.

Assume further that over the term of the loan, this family would also pay $150,000 in interest. In addition, the family would likely pay another $150,000 for maintenance, taxes, insurance, and other expenses related to the house. That's a combined $450,000 for shelter, including the original cost of $150,000.

The housing costs sound outrageous, but compute the combined amount of food and clothing over this same period. Keeping the amount conservatively at $30,000 per year ($20,000 food plus $10,000 clothing), the cost of these items would come to $900,000, or twice the cost of the housing.

Additionally, the $150,000 home would most likely appreciate over the thirty-year period, quite possibly doubling to $300,000, thereby offsetting much of the total costs of home ownership. In this example, an appreciation of $150,000 would reduce the total cost of the home from $450,000 to $300,000. Under this assumption, the food, clothing, and personal effects would triple the net costs of home ownership over a thirty-year period.

To make the point simple, food and clothing add up over time, and must always be purchased, but are consumed in shorter units of time than a house. Groceries may last two weeks. A house should last at least thirty years. Consequently, food and clothing are not compatible with debt due to their short-term nature.

A house, despite being a Maslow need, is a long-term asset that is expensive on the front end but lasts for a long period of time. This is where debt has its merit and allows many Americans to smooth out the high front-end cost of housing over many years.

Most of us never stop to consider this, but renting a house is essentially the same as making payments on a house that one personally owns. The primary difference is who legally owns the property and who is receiving the monthly payment. Furthermore, financing a home the right way can result in the eventual ownership of a viable level 5 asset to the individual.

BUYING LEVEL 2 ASSETS (SHORT-TERM)
So far, we have only considered debt in relation to level 1 assets, and we have determined that housing is the only such asset that should be financed. What about financing level 2 assets, or modern Maslow "big ticket" items such as cars and furniture? This is a difficult category to get my hands around in the way of advice, particularly in the case of automobiles.

An automobile is somewhat of a midterm asset that typically lasts for several years. On the one hand, it is similar to a house in that its high cost in most cases requires financing, especially given the fact that many households now require at least two automobiles. On the other hand, an automobile is similar to food and clothing in that it will eventually waste away. It just takes several years to do so.

In an ideal world, automobiles should never be purchased with debt because the asset is a depreciating item. However, in keeping with the practical goal of this book, we know this doesn't hold water in real life. All I have to offer here is my own practical experience dating back to when I first graduated from college.

I was very fortunate to not have to purchase a car until after I started my first job, since my parents were kind enough to give me their car when I was eighteen. It was 1982, and the car was a red '77 Thunderbird. I will never forget that first car, or the kindness shown to me from my parents. I saved for several months after starting work before making my first car purchase in 1987. I did finance the purchase, but I recall putting down 50 percent of my own money. Since then, I have made that a minimum requirement before purchasing the next vehicle.

Admittedly, this isn't something that is easy to do because it requires a strong element of financial discipline. Nevertheless, I maintain the automobile is one of two major items that significantly holds back Americans' progress in accumulating net worth.

Before I proceed further, I will stay firm that one's goal should be to pay down at least half of an automobile's cost, but I do acknowledge this is in many cases not realistic when it comes to the first vehicle purchased, or even subsequent purchases. Most of us know what it's like to face the realities of life after getting our first job. Oftentimes there are just too many demands on us financially to allow such a large down payment. However, putting down 50 percent should at least be a goal for vehicles purchased in later years after one has enjoyed more time to save.

As for the other level 2 assets, such as furniture and appliances, I am likewise of the opinion that putting down a sizable down payment is a worthy goal to have in mind as you evaluate purchasing these items. Again, this is difficult to do in one's early adult years. Fortunately, many companies have favorable financing options, offering very low interest rates in order to compete for the sale. In my opinion, the key is to avoid 100 percent financing and keep the payment terms for two years or less.

In addition, I would unequivocally recommend avoiding the purchase of furniture and appliances with a credit card, unless the intent is to pay the balance due the following month. In a previous paragraph, I mentioned the purchase of automobiles as one of the two major impediments to accumulating net worth. What is second on my list? Not surprisingly, the credit card is the culprit. As will be discussed in a later chapter, financing through the use of a credit is rarely a wise choice. The commonly used 18 percent financing rate of most credit cards is all that has to be said here. The logic is quite simple.

I hope you can sense by now that moderation is something that I hold near and dear to my financial values. As mentioned earlier, I will never hold to the idea that we should be a debt-free society. Rather, I strongly believe that wisely chosen debt can help lift us up by our own bootstraps at opportune times and allow us to enjoy some of the better things in life.

So far, I have mentioned the need to finance homes, automobiles, appliances, and furniture, particularly in the early years of one's adult life. Again, our focus is on debt used to finance and purchase levels 1 and 2 assets, or items for which we have a fairly strong need.

BUYING LEVEL 3 ASSETS (SHORT-TERM)

How about those level 3 assets, or, simply, how about those toys? In my view, these are the purchases that are devastating the financial health of so many Americans. In general, the problem goes back to what was discussed in the second chapter in that Americans want it all, and they want it right now. Lest I digress, I only wish to state here that 100 percent financing of these assets is foolish at best, and is an easy invitation to negative net worth.

How many boats have you seen for sale in the paper in November? Why is this the case? No one wants to be left behind in May when the masses head to the lakes. I cannot speak to the details of most boat financings, but I would assume that many deals are 100 percent financed, when in reality they should be financed at a maximum of 50 percent.

In so many cases, when autumn comes around the luster has worn off, or perhaps the family budget has been squeezed too tightly. Regardless, as so often is the case, many individuals buy a $20,000 boat in the spring and sell for $12,000 six months later. The result is a net cost of $8,000 for memories on the lake, with nothing to show for it next spring.

Personally, I think it is wonderful that boats are purchased, and that families and friends enjoy the water. However, I maintain that patience should be exercised to save and invest a bigger down payment on such purchases in order to avoid a major equity crash later. The same message can be applied to third cars or RVs. If the cash is there to buy, that is another matter. However, 90 percent and 100 percent financing of these kinds of assets will in general come back to haunt many families financially due to the combination of a low down payment and quick depreciation of the asset.

Buying levels 4 and 5 assets (long-term)

As for financing level 4 assets, we know that retirement investments by this definition come out of the employee's own funds, so there is no debt. Typically, the convenience of employer withholding injects a framework of discipline for the employee to systematically save for retirement from his or her wages.

However, there is a feature of 401(k) plans that warrants discussion in relation to obtaining a good source of debt. Most 401(k) plans allow an employee to borrow up to 50 percent against the underlying value of the plan's value. For instance, an employee having a 401(k) account value of $80,000 could qualify for a $40,000 loan. I personally did this about fifteen years ago to purchase an automobile and finance half of the purchase price.

The loan rate is typically tied to a fairly low benchmark, since the loan itself is safely secured by one's investment balance in the event of default. Furthermore, most loans are paid back by systematic withdrawals from one's paycheck, so the ease of payment and convenient discipline are two additional advantages.

Lastly, especially during periods of economic uncertainty in the stock market, utilizing a 401(k) loan guarantees that a portion of your portfolio will earn the equivalent of the interest rate you are paying. While the rest of your account may be losing money, the loan can ensure a 5 percent rate of return, for example.

Some people may counter this argument and ask why pay a 5 percent rate when you could get a lower rate, perhaps zero, with a car dealer. My answer to that would be two parts. For one, can you quantify how much more the dealer is charging you on the purchase price in offering the zero percent rate? More than likely, the trade-off from getting the zero rate isn't worth the additional purchase price.

Second, what's wrong with paying yourself? It isn't as if the interest is going to the administrator of the investment fund. Rather, it goes entirely back to your account. So essentially, this can be viewed as a forced savings account. In short, the 401(k) is something wise to consider when financing a large purchase, especially an automobile.

Of course, I would be remiss if I didn't mention the fact that taking these same funds out of your normal portfolio mix during the life of the loan could also mean losing out on possible gains above the 5 percent loan rate. In other words, if you left your 401(k) untouched and borrowed elsewhere, you might end up better off financially. But like so many other financial matters, this can be a guessing game.

My point is simply this: the 401(k) loan choice is easy, convenient, charges a very favorable loan rate, and guarantees a rate of return to yourself in the form of interest payments that you get to keep.

Furthermore, how about the purchase of level 5 assets, or nonretirement investments? Again, this can be publicly traded stock, investment in a privately held company, bonds, a vacation home, or perhaps farmland. Should debt be incurred to purchase such assets? If so, to what extent should debt be utilized?

Personal goods and bads

Again, I draw upon personal experience as my way of giving advice here. Approximately thirteen years ago, my wife and I came upon an opportunity to purchase farmland with my parents, who were still active in farming at the time. Being unprepared for this sudden opportunity, we chose to finance the purchase of our portion of the land at 100 percent. Conventional wisdom suggests that was a foolish move. However, the banking environment at the time was such that 100 percent financing was fairly common, especially among small community banks.

Furthermore, my comfort level with this investment was built upon three factors. For one, the purchase price of the land was too good to pass up for quality farmland. Second, despite the prices of corn and soybeans being depressed at that time, I had a view that in the near future gasoline would enter the demand side of farming in the form of ethanol production. The last factor was having a good knowledge of the investment. Since I was reared on a farm, I had a base to draw upon in making pricing and cost decisions, so I had a good comfort level plus a strong interest in the investment.

In thirteen years, this same farmland would generate a return of over 400 percent if we chose to sell today. For various reasons we hope to never sell, primarily because the income stream is so favorable now, and we would like to keep the farm in the family. In essence, through incurrence of debt, we have been able to increase the asset side of our personal net worth equation four times over the original purchase price. Additionally, since the debt has now been paid off, net worth has improved that much more.

So how do I translate my own positive experience into advice? For one, I do believe in taking measured risks with investments in which you have a good knowledge. Second, I am a firm believer in investing in products or services that do not reach too far from the realm of needs and wants in society.

As an example, I once bought stock in a company that was investing in Internet bandwidth. The company was an entity related to my employer, so I had this false sense of security that nothing could go wrong. Long story short, I lost all of my investment as the company eventually went bankrupt.

First, I erred in that I invested in something that I really didn't understand. Second, the demand for this service wasn't up to the level of supply that had already saturated the market.

Likewise, I similarly invested in common stocks during the heyday of "day trading." I enjoyed multiple quick gains on the front end, only to end up losing all of those gains and more before I eventually decided to keep my investment portfolio on a more long-term focus.

Just as the farmland expanded my net worth in a relatively short time span, the failures from my stock investments took away some of that gain in an even shorter period of time. But such is the nature of investments built upon short-term profit expectations. For every get-rich-quick story of day trading of stocks, I can assure you there are many more negative stories from others who helped fund that happy ending.

WHERE IS YOUR DEBT ATTACHED?

Ideally, all debt you have should be attached to assets that are either long-lived, such as a house, or to a nonretirement investment, such as land or stock. Please notice I said *ideally*. More *practically*, all of your debts should at a minimum be attached to your itemization of assets from chapter 3. This is more in line with reality, and would most likely include automobiles, appliances, and even toys. Though not an ideal financial profile, at least there would be assets to sell and raise cash in the event of financial distress.

Lastly, the third situation to be in, which is becoming more and more common, is to have one or more debts to which there is no underlying asset attached. In other words, this is a financial profile where consumable goods (food, clothing) and perhaps a way of life (extravagant vacations) are being financed with debt. Unfortunately for many, this becomes a downward spiral that can feed upon itself over and over as the years go by. This is truly the dead-end road where unbridled debt can lead you.

Summary Points
- *A person's debt explains what is purchased beyond one's income.*
- *A debt should never exceed the related asset's value.*
- *A way of life should never be financed through debt.*

Chapter 5 Exercise

Go back to the exercise from chapter 3 and enter below all of the debts that were listed, as well as the amounts. To the right, enter the item that was purchased with each debt. In the last column, label the item according to these three categories:

1. Long-life asset (house, stock, land, retirement investment)
2. Short-life asset (car, boat, appliances)
3. Way of life (vacations, clothing, club memberships)

Debt Description	**Amount**	**Related Asset**	**Category #**

Look at the values in the last column to assess your debt profile. If there are a lot of "3" values, this indicates serious debt issues, as there is no underlying asset attached to the debt.

The ultimate goal should be zero debt, especially in one's later stages of life. But if debt is there, the ideal profile is to have underlying long-life assets.

CHAPTER 6

Hang with Me

CONVENTIONAL WISDOM SUGGESTS THAT a book about personal finances should focus upon giving concrete bits of advice, much like following a recipe book. In all honesty, my goal in beginning this book was just that, and to a large extent that hasn't changed.

However, I ask you to step aside with me for just a minute and perform a visual exercise. Imagine having ten stalks of celery lying on the kitchen table. Further, each of these stalks represents a friend in your life. You have been given the task of giving financial advice to your ten friends through the writing of a book.

Further, your cast of friends is made up of differences such as gender, career, education, age, medical hardships, and size of family. Effectively, each of these factors is the same as taking a kitchen knife and cutting a swath across all of the ten stalks simultaneously. If you do this nine times, you no longer have ten pieces of celery, but rather you have one hundred, each representing a unique combination of the characteristics just mentioned matched with each of the individuals.

To put this example into simpler terms, it makes no sense to attempt writing a book of financial advice that caters to each of the one hundred types of possible personalities and situations. To do so would, at best, end up with a monstrosity of a book, and at worst bore readers to tears with countless detail.

Our approach so far has centered upon getting us to stop and think in broad, somewhat philosophical terms in relation to personal finance. To briefly summarize, we have discussed *needs and wants*, the *measurement of current net worth*, and what makes up that worth in the form of our *assets and liabilities*. It is now that I truly hope to be able to get into the concrete issues that I feel may be of help, and which can hopefully provide the most tangible value.

The title to this chapter is a bit out of the norm. However, the object of this book is not to impress anyone with trendy titles but rather to try and reach out and keep one's interest in the matter at hand. So, as the chapter title suggests, hang with me as we move to more of the "what ifs" of financial issues.

If you will allow me to use a sports analogy from my days in high school, our basketball team spent the greater part of September and October going to the track to see where we were in terms of physical conditioning. It would have done little good to have discussed the details of a full-court press on the first day of practice if our team didn't first have the physical conditioning to execute the defense. Our coach knew we first had an intermediate goal of fitness to attain.

Once we achieved physical fitness, it was then that we were ready to move on and learn the plays for offense and defense. Being in shape by late October wasn't our goal. If so, we should have instead waited for spring to join the track team. Rather, our goal was to be the best basketball team we could be, which required the next step of learning and executing the plays to the best of our abilities.

In financial terms, we are now ready to open the play book and see what can be applied to our everyday lives. And in "celery talk," it discusses the stalks of celery one at a time rather than trying to bombard you with advice that would attempt to cover those one hundred combinations.

Remember simplicity, and you will never go wrong.

Chapter 7

Investments and Insurance

THE CONCEPT OF INVESTMENTS is a topic that I believe I could find a way to write ten thousand words about, and in the end not really put together anything of substantial value. Having said that, I have just opened myself up to criticism as to why I have chosen to add insurance to the chapter, seemingly making the task that much more difficult.

Ironically, I found through the writing of this chapter that investments and insurance are two very similar subjects that are relied upon to achieve the same objective—financial security. Admittedly, it is quite difficult to give specific advice as to what investments to make and how much insurance to purchase. However, I have found to my surprise that discussing the two topics together can give one a better insight in planning one's overall financial strategy.

DISABILITY INSURANCE
First of all, I wish to make it clear that I will be referring in general to life insurance in this chapter, and that will be my primary focus as I attempt to tie this topic to the concept of investing. However, I would be remiss if I did not stress one facet of insurance that I feel is sorely overlooked today, and that is disability insurance.

In addition to health insurance, it seems that life insurance is the one type of coverage that we all seem to focus upon when we reach our young adult years. Even many of the most financially undisciplined individuals stop and consider what coverage they need. I have an unproven theory as to why this might be the case, and like other opinions that I share, this theory is partly based upon my own experiences.

I distinctly recall being at Murray State University during the last week of my final semester in May 1986 and receiving a call from a local insurance agent wanting to sell life insurance. To this day, I can picture myself sitting in the lobby of Hart Hall dormitory listening to this guy offering me his sales pitch. I do not recall the specifics of the conversation, but I do know that I didn't purchase the insurance. Perhaps it was because I knew I had a job waiting for me with this benefit.

But twenty-six years later this I do know: life insurance is a profitable business for the insurance companies, and they especially want to insure the young adult segment. Why? Because the insurance companies have the mortality tables on their side to support premiums yielding almost guaranteed profits. After the agent who met with me left that day, who do you think he met next? Do you think he met an eighty-five-year-old widow down the street, or another student getting ready to leave college with statistically many years left to live? You know the answer.

I mention that story to stress this fact. Young adults in particular, while needing life insurance, probably need disability insurance even more. This is especially true in today's generation where many young adults are waiting longer to marry and have families. Between high school graduation and marriage, I venture to say many young men and women spend numerous weekends doing things such as water skiing, motorcycle riding, running, and other types of active and sometimes dangerous recreation.

As much as we like to think "it will never be me," unfortunate injuries do happen all the time, some of which can have a serious impact upon one's ability to earn a living.

On a personal level, I played *competitive* basketball from my early years through high school. The only injury I experienced during those years was a sprained ankle. Between the ages of twenty-three and forty-one, I broke my nose and tore both of my knee ligaments, all playing *recreational* basketball. Fortunately, I had a career where the knee injuries in particular didn't interfere with my ability to perform my job.

The point in mentioning this is that a young adult, especially one still single, should perhaps put disability insurance at a priority above life insurance, at least until a spouse or child comes into the picture. After all, if one is single, who is it that needs the life insurance protection? Unless one's parents need the protection, I recommend that disability insurance be given the higher priority. After all, it is a statistical game as to which is more likely, death or an injury that can hamper one's career.

LIFE INSURANCE

Now, in moving the focus back to life insurance, I hope to make the topics of investments and insurance much simpler and less intimidating than most people view them. To a large extent life is all about managing the financial demands in purchasing level 1 and level 2 assets, those things needed to survive. Additionally, living in modern-day society, we enjoy purchasing the level 3 toys as well.

If you are one who has already begun a career, have you ever stopped to think what your *long-term* financial goal should be? A common answer would be to retire early, and with lots of money. However, let's take this back a step further and question what one's more immediate goal should be.

Very simply, a person's *most immediate* financial goal is to meet his or her family's everyday needs of food, clothing, and housing. That is where the first dollars of the paycheck go. But is there an *intermediate* goal between daily survival and a long-term goal of retiring at age sixty-five? Without realizing it, most of us begin a career and then proceed to (1) plan for the planned, and (2) plan for the unplanned.

In planning for the planned, or retirement, what we are really doing is coming up with a strategy so that when we reach a certain age we will have the financial means to continue purchasing our needs and wants, minus the demands of a job. During our careers, we are essentially funding needs and wants in the present as well as funding needs and wants many years out. Funding for future purchases comes primarily in the form of level 4 assets, such as 401(k) and IRA investments, and ideally includes level 5 assets as one accumulates additional net worth later in life.

Planning for the unplanned, or *death*, is where we set aside money to purchase life insurance that will serve as a backstop in the event of death. Assuming a young individual who is married with a child, an untimely death can take away more than forty years of wage potential, easily adding up to more than $2 million of lost support for the family left behind. To turn one's back on such a possibility is the same as ignoring reality. The thought is not pleasant, but the financial result can be disastrous.

So what should be the optimal mix of investments and insurance? If you think in terms of financial commitments to needs and wants, this really isn't a hard question to answer. Imagine that you are looking at a seesaw from a side view. A small child gets on the left side and is sitting at ground level. As an analogy, this represents the financial position of a typical young adult just starting a career and a family.

Perhaps one's bottom being on the ground is symbolic here. Are financial obligations present in the form of needs and wants? Indeed they are. Hopefully, the individual will have the earnings capacity to meet present demands. But what about future obligations coming before retirement such as college education, and what about those obligations that may continue even after retirement?

In this situation, financial risk is high and mortality risk is low. Absent an individual having a coffer of wealth to fall back upon, the result of death could be quite traumatic to the family left behind. So what is the logical answer? Life insurance, perhaps up to $500,000, should be an objective. If you think this is out of touch with reality, recall the modest calculation of $2 million in salary that we assumed for a career of forty years. At this age, ensuring $500,000 of income protection and peace of mind is a bargain in relation to the cost of the underlying life insurance.

Assuming our hypothetical individual is twenty-five years old, let us flip forward ten years into the future. Hopefully, by this time a decent amount of savings would be accumulated in one's retirement funds. Furthermore, it is no secret that both present and future obligations would still exist, probably even more so than at age twenty-five if more children were now in the picture.

Going back to our analogy, this stage of life should at least be where the seesaw gets off the ground. This suggests that the risk profile of the individual would now shift more from financial risk to mortality risk. In other words, accumulated savings should now be greater to better provide for a rainy day. But the downside is the mortality tables begin to shift and make the life insurance more expensive.

To carry our analogy further, assume the same progression as one moves to age forty-five, and then to age fifty-five. Between each time interval, our visual of the seesaw should be of the child getting higher and higher, as retirement funds ideally continue to grow in addition to other investments. Conversely, the life insurance companies keep getting a little more nervous and increase the life insurance premiums. To do otherwise would be foolish on their part, and we would do the same.

At a desired retirement of sixty-five, the seesaw should, in a perfect world, be all the way to the top. At this position, financial risk should be low and, unfortunately, mortality risk gets closer to the high category. At retirement, one should enter his or her golden years free from housing debt and college expenses in particular, therefore being in a position to comfortably meet future needs and wants.

Just like a handoff within a relay team, the retirement funds plus Social Security now come in as the fresh set of legs to hopefully give a happy finish to one's life. Yes, in a way this sounds a bit somber, but to not plan for such a stage in life is, to me, a much sadder thought to consider.

HOW MUCH TO INSURE AND HOW LONG TO KEEP?

Investments should start early in one's career and, if possible, not be cashed out until retirement. The 10 percent early withdrawal penalty imposed upon early IRA withdrawals is not enough of a deterrent to keep individuals from taking early distributions. I have personally completed way too many tax returns for clients who have chosen to take the early distribution.

Admittedly, there are circumstances such as health and housing issues that cannot be avoided. However, for these the IRS allows one to avoid the 10 percent penalty. For other noncritical distributions, I think it would be profitable in the long run for the penalty to be at least 25 percent so that more individuals would choose not to take the early distribution option.

Never before have I given specific advice as to how one should invest in his or her retirement portfolio. Rather, I hold to the long-term view that one should diversify as much as possible, put aside as much as possible, and let the investments run their course. Also, I only reiterate here what I have heard all of my adult life. That is, in the early years invest more heavily in the equity investments that carry more risk, yet have more profit potential in the long run. As one progresses through his or her career, the portfolio should tilt more toward conservative investments that lend themselves to more stable returns and less market value fluctuations.

Regarding insurance, I do not have a specific formula for how much to insure, or how long to keep a life insurance policy active. The amount of optimal life insurance is influenced by many factors, including annual earnings, health of family members, college obligations, and spending lifestyle.

However, no matter the amount of the desired coverage, here is the one constant that will never fail: as one ages, the cost of coverage increases. The math is so simple, yet I often see individuals in their later years carrying way too much life insurance. Recalling the seesaw, there comes a time in a person's life when mortality risk and its cost outweigh the benefit of any life insurance payout.

For instance, at age twenty-five the annual cost of a $100,000 life insurance policy can be purchased for as little as $50. Most of us think what a great deal that is. On the other hand, what would a similar policy cost for a ninety-year-old person? Without getting an actual price quote, I would think such a policy would approach $50,000. At that rate, an insurance company could break even if this individual lived approximately two years. It sounds outrageous, but would you quote anything less if you were the insurance company?

The point to be made is that after a certain stage in life, it is more profitable to take the money that would be spent on life insurance and invest in something besides your life expectancy. In my opinion, a long-term nursing care policy would put those funds to better use, as nursing home expenses can be astronomical over an extended period of time. If nothing else, tucking the money under a mattress would probably be a better option than life insurance.

Going back to the $500,000 policy example, I would in general maintain this would be a good amount of insurance to keep through age fifty. After this age, one should ideally begin to scale back on coverage, much of that depending upon how free of debt the individual is. If one is employed during this stage, relying only upon the coverage funded by the employer gives the best of all worlds.

My personal goal is to have no need for life insurance by retirement age of sixty-five. Whether I get to that level of comfort by then, only time will tell. But if I were forced to give someone simple advice, I would recommend a minimum of $500,000 coverage during one's early adult years, and a goal of zero coverage by age sixty-five.

In summary, I go back to the seesaw from our earlier example. Given the mathematics of mortality tables, we all are given a number of good years to lean upon life insurance companies as a cheap source of financial backstop. In essence, they become the retirement payout when the worst happens.

Once the seesaw levels off, where I currently exist in my life, the insurance company starts to become the enemy in financial terms. This is where lack of financial discipline will expose many who do not properly set aside money for retirement, as a life insurance policy should never be your best retirement option. If so, it will eventually rob you of everything you have worked for in your life. So focus on saving early, saving often, and saving wisely. You will never regret that you did.

Summary Points
- *Do not forget disability insurance when planning your insurance needs.*
- *Life insurance is simply "planning for the unplanned," or death.*
- *Investment goals should be to "plan for the planned," or retirement.*
- *Younger years should rely more upon life insurance; later years should rely more upon investments.*

Chapter 7 Exercise

List all life and disability insurance policies you currently have, identifying amount of coverage as well as annual cost. (Cost per $1,000 = annual cost x $1,000 divided by coverage). This will give you a good basis to compare the costs among insurance companies.

***Type of insurance*:**

D = Disability L = Life	Amount of coverage	Your annual cost	Cost per $1,000
1.____	_____	_____	_____
2.____	_____	_____	_____
3.____	_____	_____	_____
4.____	_____	_____	_____
5.____	_____	_____	_____
6.____	_____	_____	_____

Now, sum the total amounts of coverage by type listed above:
Disability _____
Life _____

Based on your age and level of debt, do you feel your insurance coverage is adequate? In your years of peak need for coverage, anything less than $500,000 should be evaluated and seriously questioned.

CHAPTER 8

Insurance: Term or Whole?

HEALTH, DISABILITY, LIFE, THEFT, automobile, property, and liability are all types of insurance that most Americans cannot avoid. Whether we realize it or not, we as individuals fund these kinds of "bad news" costs over our lifetime. The large insurance companies are just the collectors of these funds from individuals, and they make a good living paying the money when needed. Essentially, insurance companies are here for us to smooth out the cost of life's bad events.

In the prior chapter, life insurance was discussed in relation to its purpose in ensuring financial security in the event of untimely death. However, the preferred choice is obviously enjoying a normal life and achieving financial security through wise investing.

Just like all parts of our life, insurance is no different than buying any other need or want. In the United States, marketing has been and will always be alive and well. Consequently, we stay bombarded with choices beyond what we really need. Here is a prime example: it is quite common that when I purchase something as simple as a twenty-five-dollar toaster, I am asked at the checkout counter if I would like to purchase a three-dollar warranty.

Is this because corporate America cares about me so much it wants to make sure I am protected to the fullest? At the risk of sounding negative, my answer is a definite no. Instead, marketing researchers have done enough work to know that many warranties that are purchased never get registered or get misplaced, or perhaps if something goes wrong many consumers just go buy another product. Therefore, the three dollars is a way to pad the profit margin on the sale.

Life insurance likewise takes on a variety of creative marketing in the form of *whole life* insurance policies. When interest rates were quite high in the late 1970s and early 1980s, I remember whole life insurance being quite common. Nowadays, I don't hear about this as much, so I don't know if it is selective hearing on my part, or if the financial environment just isn't as favorable today for this type of investment.

How Whole Life Works

Basically, whole life insurance is asking not just for the assurance of financial security at death, but also the achievement of financial security while one is still living in the form of an investment account. If this sounds too good to be true, the quick answer is that indeed it is.

A whole life policy will obviously cost more than traditional *term life* due to the investment piece of the package. For example, a typical $100,000 term policy might cost $450 per year for a person my age, while the whole life option could cost $700. Doing simple subtraction, the $250 difference is the portion of funds that would be set aside and invested by the insurance company under the whole life option.

Obviously, the attractiveness of the whole life option is the projected buildup of the investment account, commonly referred to as *cash surrender value*. For someone starting at an early age, an insurance agent can quote some very impressive investment numbers for a projected retirement age. A few decades ago, the principle worked something similar to this: the insurance company would guarantee an investment rate of perhaps 4 percent, then take your extra $250 for the investment piece and earn a yield of 15 percent in the stock market. The spread of 11 percent would be money in the pockets of the insurance companies.

Furthermore, as one ages, a greater proportion of the $700 premium used in our example goes toward the insurance protection, leaving less money to put toward the investment. In fact, at a certain stage the $700 no longer becomes enough for the life insurance, so the insurance company starts tapping into the cash surrender value. Until one chooses to cash out the policy, the insurance company has tremendous leverage in having access to the funds to ensure payment of the annual premium. Meanwhile, if coverage remains intact, the cash surrender value will gradually begin to erode as the required additional premium eventually exceeds the annual earnings on the investment.

WHICH ROAD TO TAKE?

Going back to the seesaw once again, there comes a point when one must decide whether to keep the investment (plan for the planned) or hold to the insurance (plan for the unplanned). The mortality tables will eventually dictate that both objectives can exist for only a limited amount of time.

My general advice regarding life insurance is to choose term coverage rather that whole life. From our example, I suggest paying the $450 for the protection, and investing the $250 in something of one's own choosing. The insurance company was paying 4 percent and earning 15 percent. If the individual could instead invest the extra $250 and earn an average of 7 percent, he or she would come out with a much greater investment balance years down the road.

Keep in mind this example is using hypothetical rates that are undoubtedly above the market rates today. However, the principle still holds true whether the guaranteed whole life rate is 4 percent, or as low as 1 percent. It only makes sense that where a middleman (life insurance company) exists, one's rate of return will generally be impacted in the negative direction.

Furthermore, buying term insurance and investing the difference yourself is only good advice if both pieces of the advice are executed. For instance, buying the insurance protection for $450 and then blowing the $250 on something frivolous is almost the worst of all actions to take. The only thing worse would be taking the full

$700 each year and turning one's back completely on insurance and investment responsibilities.

Before I put this topic to rest, I do wish to interject a realistic exception to the advice just shared. For whatever reason, if an individual is not disciplined enough to buy term and invest the difference, I believe that a whole life policy is the proper choice.

After all, this will at least ensure that for a limited amount of time the individual will be protected with life insurance and have an investment to fall back upon if needed. I do not agree with the logic or the lack of financial discipline. However, I have at least made my one case for choosing whole life insurance. Sometimes it does pay to have a warranty on a toaster.

Summary Points
- *Whole life coverage tries to give the best of both worlds, but cannot.*
- *Ideally, one should purchase term insurance and invest the difference.*
- *Worst case, one who lacks financial discipline may be better with whole life.*

Chapter 8 Exercise

Go back to the chapter 7 exercise and evaluate each of the life insurance policies and determine if any are whole life. If so, enter information below.

Whole life payout at death	Current cash surrender value balance	Annual premium
1.		
2.		
3.		
4.		
5.		
6.		

From this exercise, consider the following:
1. Is the whole life policy expensive compared to term? If so, evaluate changing coverage to term.
2. Is the annual policy premium locked in for an extended period of time? If the cost isn't expensive, perhaps keeping the policy in place is the right choice for now.
3. Do you have significant cash surrender values? If so, cashing the policy and paying down debt could be the best use of the money. Look back to your list of debts from the exercise in chapter 5. Do you have a high-rate

Fields of Green | 53

debt, perhaps a credit card balance? Paying down high-interest debt with the cash surrender value would be a wise use of funds, followed by replacing the whole life policy with a term policy.

CHAPTER 9

College Funding

IN KEEPING WITH THE theme of investments, I would be negligent if I didn't devote some time to the topic of funding a college education. In my adult years, this area of financial planning has quickly emerged into one of the three or four major hurdles that challenge our ultimate retirement goal. So much has changed in the last thirty years that it borders on being scary.

In 1982, I attended Madisonville Community College for two years before later earning my accounting degree at Murray State. To this day, I recall the tuition bill for that fall semester, which was a mind-boggling $144. For younger readers, this wasn't per credit hour, but rather the $144 was the tuition for the entire semester!

Though I wasn't by any means rich at the time, I was able to comfortably fund my first two years as well as my final years at Murray State with the money from my tobacco crops. Just as a side note, though my accounting education at Murray was top notch, my experience in that tobacco patch was truly the best education I ever received. I highly recommend it to anyone.

Fortunately, I was able to earn my undergraduate degree about five years before the cost increases in college education began to really have an impact. In the early 1990s, universities were suddenly increasing tuition costs at about 10 percent per year, and this is just from my recollection of state schools in Kentucky. In general, the decreases in state funding, increased demand for college degrees, and the need to update university infrastructures all contributed to the sudden escalation in costs.

Though 10 percent may sound innocent enough, seven consecutive years of such increases effectively amount to a 100 percent increase. Add those same percentage increases over another seven-year period, and you have another doubling of costs. So essentially, in a fifteen-year period of time, it was not uncommon to see state college costs quadruple. I'm sure many other folks, especially in private universities, could attest to much greater increases.

COLLEGE SAVINGS PLANS

In response to the huge increases in education costs, there have been a variety of actions taken to help mitigate the increases. Among these have been education plans offered by states as well as section 529 plans. The state plans work in such a way that money set aside now to pay for college expenses later will generate tax-free earnings at both the state and federal level. The main drawback with some of the state plans is the eventual selection of a school must be one within the particular state of choice. The section 529 plans work much the same way, but they don't restrict where one can attend college.

These plans really gained popularity in the mid-to-late 1990s, as this was a time of very good returns in the stock market. These funds were, therefore, favorably looked upon as a way to match inflationary education costs with the added advantage of tax-free earnings. One primary drawback, however, was the restriction on the eventual uses of the funds, particularly the earnings that were being given tax-free treatment.

For instance, what if after a decade of funding the account, the child received a full scholarship? In this case, the distributions of earnings from the fund would be treated as taxable for any noneducation purpose, thereby taking away one of the advantages of the investment. Also, what if the child decided not to attend college? Again, any earnings distributions would have to be reported as taxable income.

Education Tax Credits

Another popular means of alleviating education costs came in 1998 in the form of education tax credits. In my opinion, this has been one of the smarter things that our leaders in Washington have done over the past several years. In general, with variations of the tax break made since its inception, the federal government has allowed families to either claim a tax credit or a tax deduction on the parents' tax returns. The current credit stands at $2,500 per child, though obviously for most families this falls way short of the actual education costs per year.

The positive side of these credits has been that families are not restricted in setting up a separate fund for education, and second, the nature of a tax credit is the equivalent of a dollar-for-dollar reduction in the cost of education. This is in contrast to the education plans that offer only tax-free treatment of the investment earnings.

The downside of the credits and education deductions, however, is that for higher-income families the benefit of the credits or deductions can be partially or totally phased out if adjusted gross income exceeds certain threshold amounts.

Similar to being asked investment advice, education funding has likewise been an area where there are too many situational "what ifs" to make me comfortable in giving a set answer. Again, so many factors have to be taken into account, most notably income level, ambitions of the child, the child's prospect for scholarships, and one's comfort level in choosing investments for the education funds.

From my general observation, it appears the 1990s was the decade of high confidence in the investment market for education funding, whereas the past decade has been one where many education funds have really taken a hit from the volatility in the stock market, especially those funds invested heavily in the high-tech industries around the turn of the century.

On a personal level, I have observed a tax client's son making perfect use of the education fund to where virtually all of his education was provided, and largely through the help of his grandparent. This highlights one of the advantages of the education plans. However, it has been my general observation from preparing tax returns over the past several years that the utilization of the education credits has been the more common choice, perhaps due to less complexity and more flexibility.

All of the advantages and disadvantages of the education plans and tax credits only underscore the fact that the impact of educational costs has been dramatic over the past two decades. During a time when the need to fund retirement plans has increased, the pressure to meet future college obligations has effectively created another version of a pension to fund. For families with several children, the total cash outlay can approximate several hundred thousand dollars.

COLLEGE SAVINGS PLAN OR TAX CREDITS? JUST SAVE

Ironically, my general advice for educational funding is about as simple as you can get. That is, set aside money early in the child's life. Ideally, the money should be put in the child's name, whether it is in the form of a simple investment (perhaps a savings account), or set up as an education fund.

The secondary objective is to keep the income from being taxed at the parents' level, if practical. Even if an education fund isn't set up, a child can make up to $950 each year on ordinary investments with no tax consequence. Therefore, especially in the early years, either option should have no tax impact unless huge amounts of money are being set aside on behalf of the child.

Personally, my wife and I made the choice a few years ago to choose the tax credit in addition to regular savings as our strategy for funding college for Savannah, our daughter, and Cameron, our son, who will graduate high school in the years 2013 and 2017, respectively. The downside risk of this approach is there is never any guarantee as to how long a tax break will remain in place. However, in the case of education, I don't feel the lawmakers will be willing to take this away from the American public, for both political and economic reasons.

Furthermore, our specific strategy of funding our children's education was tied to the timing of the anticipated payoff of our home mortgage in 2010. It was our initial goal that the amount formerly paid for housing each month would immediately start going to an account set up for Savannah. This way, the impact would be negligible, yet the accumulation of funds by fall 2013 would be significant.

However, in early 2010 we came upon another opportunity to buy farmland adjacent to our existing farm. Though not quite the deal that we enjoyed on the earlier purchase, I was still bullish on farmland and tied up a good deal of our money with a significant down payment. Despite the fact that my initial strategy changed, we nevertheless have a funding plan that I feel will be as effective if not more so than the original plan.

Specifically, we have chosen to allocate all of the farm earnings to the education needs of the children starting in 2013, if not before. This isn't anything complicated at all. In fact, it is downright simple. The farm earnings, representing a fairly stable source of annual income, will be relied upon to meet all of the education expenses for at least eight years of college. However, if discipline isn't practiced, the strategy is worth no more than the piece of paper you are reading.

Just like funding a pension, or saving for a house, or saving to buy a farm, the end result of success can occur only if proper planning and action both take place. In being able to share with you my strategy for funding college, I take a sense of pride in that we are beginning to see the rewards of our financial discipline over the past twenty-five years.

If not for choosing to sacrifice some of our wants in the earlier years, we would never have accumulated the acres of farmland that will generate earnings for the rest of our lives. Looking back, we could have chosen to spend those dollars on toys, but where would those be now? And further, even if we still had them, what kind of financial return would they be generating?

Funding for college doesn't have to be sophisticated and doesn't necessarily require a tax-free strategy, nor must it involve investments in companies listed on the New York Stock Exchange. Instead, the age-old virtues of planning, patience, and financial sacrifice will take a family quite far in helping to meet educational costs.

Additionally, I would be remiss if I didn't add that children helping to fund the costs through their own sweat equity, no matter how small that might be, is very important in establishing a level of commitment to achieving a college education. The financial commitment is far too serious to not have both parents and children pulling in the same direction.

Summary Points
- *College funding today is essentially the same as planning a retirement fund.*
- *Too often parents put off proper planning, and the result is huge long-term debt.*
- *Wise use of college tuition plans and tax credits can at least help offset high education costs.*
- *Start saving now, and save as much as you can. There is no sophisticated secret.*

Chapter 9 Exercise

Estimate your future college obligations for your children using the format below.

Child's name	Current age	Total Cost estimates	Less expected scholarships	Net cost
1._____	___	_____	_____	_____
2._____	___	_____	_____	_____
3._____	___	_____	_____	_____
4._____	___	_____	_____	_____
5._____	___	_____	_____	_____
6._____	___	_____	_____	_____
Totals		_____	_____	_____

Now go back to the net worth exercise from chapter 3 and identify any assets you listed that will be available to pay toward your estimated college costs. If you are sorely underfunded and your children are young, you at least have time to implement a savings strategy. The important point from this exercise is to stop and evaluate where you are in relation to future college obligations, and then take action accordingly.

Fields of Green

CHAPTER 10

Tax Avoidance: Don't Get Carried Away

ONE OF THE VERY first things I learned in studying tax in college was the difference between *tax evasion* and *tax avoidance*. Both involve the same goal of not paying tax, but tax evasion is the sort of strategy that can put one behind bars. On the other hand, tax avoidance is by definition the goal of minimizing one's taxes within legal means.

One of the simplest examples of tax avoidance is the shifting of income and/or deductions between two periods in order to keep taxable income below the next higher tax bracket. A self-employed person in particular has the flexibility to prepay expenses at the end of a tax year if he or she feels his or her taxable income is otherwise going to be above the threshold for the higher tax bracket. It really boils down to simple mathematics and allocating income efficiently between tax years.

However, just like most things in life, what one takes away or adds to one period has the opposite effect in the following year. That is, the self-employed person who prepays expenses at the end of year one to avoid tax will find himself in year two having less expense to deduct than if he or she had not made the prepayment. But carefully done, tax avoidance can be an effective way to increase one's net worth by simply reducing total tax payments to the government.

REACTIVE APPROACH TO OPPORTUNITIES AND TAXES

What I would like to discuss now is what I refer to as the negative side of tax avoidance. Specifically, I feel that some people turn their backs on potential opportunities because of an overemphasis on the tax impact of earning additional income.

I have heard the phrase "but the taxes will kill you" so many times when listening to individuals discuss the thought of taking on a secondary job or making a financial investment. In fact, it seems some people are more drawn to engage in activities that will generate a deductible loss, thereby reducing income and tax. This is why the IRS has rules designed to prevent tax losses from activities determined to be hobbies rather than legitimate businesses.

Granted, there are times when one should be especially cautious in considering the tax impact of generating additional income. Two common situations come to mind that warrant careful attention. First, individuals who are drawing disability payments and those who receive Social Security benefits before full retirement age must be very careful as to how much *earned income* they receive, which is basically noninvestment income such as wages.

Specifically, those receiving disability payments are not entitled to any earned income, as this can risk losing all disability benefits. For nondisability Social Security retirees, this can be a bit trickier, as individuals between the ages of sixty-two and the applicable full retirement age (generally sixty-six or sixty-seven) can make earned income, but only up to a certain limit. Above this threshold, currently at $14,460 for 2012, the benefits are taken away on a pro rata basis. In this case, $1 of benefit is lost for each $2 above the threshold.

Keep in mind here this isn't so much a *taxation* issue as it is a *loss of benefits* issue. Also, a further distinction should be noted that the loss of benefits for one disabled can be permanent, whereas the loss of benefits for a Social Security retiree would pertain only to the year when earned income was above the allowed threshold.

Second, contemplating the receipt of additional income should be considered when a higher level of adjusted gross income can trigger certain benefits being taxed at a higher percentage. The prime example here is again Social Security benefits for retirees. In general, lower-income taxpayers are not taxed on these benefits. However, for adjusted gross incomes in excess of $25,000 for single taxpayers, and above $32,000 for married taxpayers filing jointly, the issue of taking in additional income should be carefully considered.

Without getting into tax complexities, the formula for assessing the taxability of one's Social Security benefits is such that an additional income of $5,000, for example, could trigger a tax impact of approximately $2,500 just on the federal return. Thus, the additional income of $5,000 would carry with it an effective tax rate of 50 percent, perhaps suggesting to the taxpayer that the efforts of generating the additional income wouldn't be worth keeping only half after taxes.

Similarly, the consequences of additional income can in certain circumstances trigger high effective income tax rates as a result of losing college education credits, child credits, and other such tax incentives that have their eligibility and benefit phased out as adjusted gross income increases above the defined threshold. Unfortunately, these are often tax traps that do not become visible until the year end is closed, and the tax preparer is assessing one's tax situation.

As a way of advice, I would recommend anyone receiving Social Security benefits or tax credits to consider these taxability issues in November or December of each year. This ensures at least a consideration of options which would lower the current taxable income and help lower Social Security taxability or preserve valuable tax credits. Indeed, a tax practitioner's true value is somewhat limited if you wait and ask questions after December 31.

Proactive approach

Going back to the negative side of tax avoidance, I have often jokingly stated that I would gladly accept someone else's income even if it carried a 90 percent tax rate. Think about it. Would you take on $10,000 without any extra effort and pay $9,000 in tax?

In fact, I would beg to take on every such deal that I could get my hands on.

This is obviously an exaggerated example, but the same applies in a more realistic situation in life. For example, if an individual has the potential to have a side career doing something he or she enjoys and is good at, why wouldn't that individual pursue that opportunity in order to make more money? If the answer is family time doesn't want to be sacrificed, that is a very good reason. However, if the impact of taxes is the concern, then I feel this is a very shortsighted reason for not pursuing something that could be a source of financial gain and fulfillment.

Personally, I feel a big issue in one's contemplation of generating additional income is pricing the product or service too low. Admittedly, I struggle with this myself, especially when it comes to charging fees to friends and family for tax services. However, one should generally not charge customers a price that doesn't take into account all costs of doing business, and that includes the effects of income tax.

On the flip side of this, you as a customer of a phone company help pay that company's income tax each month that you pay your bill. If, for instance, your charge is $100, you can bet that $10 to $20 of your payment is going to help cover the tax impact of that company making profitable income. If the phone company can recover its income taxes, why shouldn't you?

One should also be cautious of establishing a billing rate that just comes off the top of your head, or is simply an amount that you've heard charged in the area. After all, who is to say your service isn't better? Ideally, with a small investment of time you should sit down and calculate what your billing rate needs to be, including an amount to cover income taxes. The key point is to not underestimate the value of your service, as it is much easier to reduce the billing rate later rather than go in the other direction.

To go a step further, a well-priced service will only be as good as one's level of financial discipline in planning for the eventual payment of the income taxes. For instance, employees are "fortunate" in that they have financial discipline forced upon them in the form of required federal and state tax withholdings. Of course, our beloved governments aren't trying to do employees any favor by withholding the tax. Rather, we all know that governments have bills to pay as well and cannot wait until US citizens file their tax returns the next year.

How serious would it be if the federal government gave employees the option to receive wages in full during the year and settle their taxes by the following April 15? What percentage of the employee population do you feel would do the right thing and set aside the proper tax money? My estimate is 25 percent at best. So the governments are only acting in their own self-interests to grab their piece of the pie as wages are paid.

My point in saying all of this is that one's plan to properly consider income taxes should further include a plan to set aside the funds to pay the taxes due to come later. If properly done, the eventual tax impact should be transparent when the tax returns are filed. Paying quarterly estimates throughout the year is the obvious solution.

Again, to turn one's back on good opportunities to grow personally and financially should rarely be done in the name of tax avoidance. Unfortunately, taxes will always be around to throw a little damper on most financial gains that come our way.

Remember, tax evasion is the short-term solution to decreasing taxes that will most likely turn you into a user of those tax monies behind bars. So never resort to such a blind strategy. On the other hand, tax avoidance simply requires standing back every year in late fall to assess your situation, particularly if you happen to be self-employed.

Lastly, remember that our financial goal should be to increase net worth and not necessarily to avoid taxes. It is nearly impossible to increase the one and avoid the other. Personally, I enjoy sleeping well at night, so there is some merit in paying your proper share of tax.

Summary Points
- ***Tax evasion is illegal, while tax avoidance is a strategy to efficiently manage one's taxes.***

- *A common tax avoidance strategy is to accelerate paying expenses in one year, lowering taxable income.*
- *Poor income/deduction planning can result in loss of Social Security benefits or loss of tax credits.*
- *Income taxes should never stand in the way of pursuing good investment opportunities.*

CHAPTER 10 EXERCISE

A very qualified welder who works for a manufacturing company is considering opening his own shop to perform small jobs on weekends. Since the talent pool for welders is getting scarce, he considers this to be a good opportunity to capture additional income. Based on personal experience, he knows the direct cost of operating a welding machine typically runs $20 per hour. Since he considers clearing $40 per hour to be a good profit, he plans to price his service at $60 per hour.

Do you consider this to be a reasonable approach to valuing his service to the market? Do you think all relevant factors have been considered?

Answer:
At a minimum, it can be said that income taxes have been completely ignored in this analysis. The following simple calculation will help ensure the individual truly earns a market return:

Current service rate	$60 ($40 profit plus $20 direct expenses)
Calculated income tax at 25 percent	$10 (25 percent times $40 per hour profit)
Revised service rate should be	$70 (current rate of $60 + $10 to recover taxes)

Though the above calculation isn't exactly accurate, the point to be made is that instead of charging $60 per hour, the welder should charge $70 in order to eventually net the $40 per hour he is seeking, after payment of $20 in direct costs and $10 of income tax.

Remember the importance of better estimating the value of your services. Though not readily apparent, proper pricing will help ensure that you maximize your net worth as you invest your human capital, especially in a vocation that you consider fulfilling.

CHAPTER 11

'Tis Better to Receive—Part I

ALONG THE LINE OF taxes, I now wish to discuss one area that has probably been asked of me more than any other topic. Specifically, I am asked quite often how much money one can receive without having to pay income tax. Notice that I didn't say money *earned*, but rather money *received*. This is where the source of most of the confusion lies.

As for income earned, I think in general most individuals realize that everyone, including children, is allowed a certain level of income to be exempt from tax. The size of the exempt amount varies depending upon age of the taxpayer, marital and dependency status, and whether employed. Without bogging the discussion down with details of tax law, I will simply say it is common that adult individuals and families can earn their first $10,000 to $15,000 free of federal income tax.

RECEIVING PROPERTY

The area I wish to narrow the focus upon is *receiving* money and property, and the tax impact upon both the *one giving*, or *donor*, and the *one receiving* the gift, or *donee*. For the most part, the questions come from those who are either about to receive a gift or have already received the amount in question. For these people, I give the answer that so often sounds too good to be true, which is the receipt of the gift triggers no tax liability to the donee.

As I explain my answer, I try to make sure such an individual is aware that only the future income that will come his or her way because of the gift will carry any tax consequence. For example, if you receive a $20,000 cash gift at the beginning of the year and invest in a 2 percent savings account, the only tax impact to you in that year will be a $400 increase in your taxable income from the additional interest. Recalling our past chapter on tax avoidance, this is one of those situations where I would gladly take on the tax responsibilities in return for the $20,000 gift.

Now you may be wondering what the downside is to such a good news story. After all, we have just confirmed the donee does not have to report the $20,000 received as income. We are so conditioned to thinking in terms of when receiving money, there is always a tax consequence. But in this case, the money received isn't income, but rather is nontaxable property in the form of cash.

On the flip side, it is natural to conclude that the downside of this asset transfer must then fall on the donor, which seems a bit contradictory since this person is supposedly the good guy in the $20,000 transaction. In a general sense, this is indeed the case. However, an explanation of the way this works involves a discussion of how the federal estate and gift tax interact with one another. Again, the goal here is to avoid detailed complexities and focus on the big picture.

Overview of the Estate Tax

Starting with the federal estate tax, this has been a part of the US tax system since the early 1900s. Basically, this is a tax on net worth, much like a property tax. However, whereas the normal property tax is local and state based and is assessed while one is living, the estate tax is assessed on the value of net assets at death. The tax is confined to estates that have a large accumulation of wealth, which is currently defined as anything over $5.1 million for federal purposes. Depending upon the state of jurisdiction, estates less than $5.1 million may be subject to estate tax at the state level.

Going back to the federal tax, the exemption was only $600,000 as recently as 1997, so I would advise anyone to not get too comfortable with the large exemption currently in place. In fact, barring legislative extension in late 2012, the $5.1 million is scheduled to be reduced to $1.0 million in 2013.

Just like income tax, the estate tax can be open to some effective tax avoidance strategies that are within the boundaries of tax law. If $5.1 million is the exemption ($10.2 million if married), then good common sense would indicate that an elderly individual or married couple would strive to keep their net worth at or below the exemption amount if possible. This is where the strategy of *gifting*, or transfer of wealth before death, comes into play.

To make this as simple as possible, an individual can give money or other property up to an annual amount of $13,000 to as many people as he or she wishes without any estate or gift tax consequence. Furthermore, for a married couple, one spouse can give $13,000 to as many people as he or she wishes, and the other spouse can do the same. It makes no difference whether the recipients of the gifts are related to the donor. For elderly people, it is common to see such gifts being made to children and grandchildren in their late stages of life.

Reporting Excess Gifts

To show the interaction of gifting and estate tax, I will use a very simple example. Assume an elderly father with significant wealth has only a daughter, and he plans to minimize estate taxes at death. If he chooses to give a check of $13,000 to his daughter in 2012, there is no impact to anyone. However, if the daughter receives a check of $25,000 from the parent, this is where the complexity begins.

In receiving $25,000, the recipient again has no tax impact to report. On the other hand, the father will have to contend with the $12,000 excess gift made over the allowed annual exclusion of $13,000 for the daughter. This will involve the filing of a gift tax return for the year 2012.

Ironically, though called a gift tax return, the process involves reporting only the excess $12,000 gifted, and no tax becomes currently due to the IRS. Rather, the reporting is more of a tracking mechanism that the IRS uses to reduce the estate tax credit corresponding to the applicable tax exemption at death. (For 2011, the tax credit on the $5 million exemption was $1.7 million, equating to a tax rate of a little less than 35 percent).

Keep this in mind, however: if the lawmakers in Washington allow the exemption to be reduced to $1.0 million in 2013 (from $5.1 million), this lower exemption minus the reduction in exemption due to excess gifting in 2012 ($12,000 excess in our example) will become the basis for calculating estate tax for deaths after 2012.

For instance, if death of the father occurs in 2013, the exemption available to the estate will be $988,000, or $1,000,000 less the $12,000 excess from 2012. It doesn't matter what the amount of the exemption was in years prior to death when gifts were made. Rather, the excess gifting will accumulate annually and be offset against the estate tax exemption effective within the year of death.

Needless to say, this is a topic that draws a lot of attention along political party lines, and, quite frankly, I have no real sense as to the future of the exemption. Though the amount has increased tremendously over the last several years, the escalating focus to better manage the federal budget will pressure lawmakers to propose reducing the exemption in hopes of raising federal revenues.

What needs to be stressed here is that the $600,000 exemption in place in 1997 had been in existence since 1976. So obviously an increase was long overdue. Today, estate values in excess of $1 million are not that uncommon, so it is safe to say this is a real challenge for a divided group of lawmakers to find a common ground for an exemption.

As mentioned, the current $5.1 million exemption combined with a top tax rate of 35 percent is unfortunately scheduled to be adjusted down to a $1.0 million exemption with a top rate of 55 percent in 2013. If this takes place, the $1.0 million exemption will be much more burdensome to estates today than the $600,000 exemption was nearly forty years ago when the value of a dollar was significantly greater.

Personally, I think there should be no estate tax at all, and this view is not grounded in any political ideologies. Rather, I feel that to pay one's share of income tax on income earned from those properties during a person's lifetime is sufficient. To then assess a federal property tax on those same assets at death, up to a maximum rate of 55 percent, is to me a strong disincentive to save for the future.

Summary Points

- *There is a huge difference between "income" and "money received."*
- *In general, income will always be taxable.*
- *Money or property received, through death or gift, is not taxable to the receiving party.*
- *The donor (giving party) must be aware of giving "excess" gifts, which is any amount above $13,000 in a given year to a particular person.*
- *This excess above $13,000 can trigger a gift tax return, though no tax will be currently due from the donor for the excess gift.*
- *Any excess gifts will eventually reduce the donor's estate tax exemption at death, possibly causing part of the estate to be taxable.*
- *Estates that are taxable and have a high proportion of noncash assets are those that typically require partial estate sales in order to generate tax money to pay the IRS.*
- *Due to legislative uncertainties, large estates warrant the advice of a tax or legal professional in helping to avoid large estate tax surprises at death to the beneficiaries.*

Chapter 12

'Tis Better to Receive ... Cash!—Part 2

To briefly summarize from the last chapter, we addressed some of the confusion as to what amounts of money can be received and the related estate tax consequences. Using gifts of $13,000 or less is an example of effective tax avoidance between parents and children, in particular, in lowering the future estate and minimizing the federal estate tax.

One other area that I see as a potential tax savings relates to what *types of assets* are given within these lifetime transfers between parent and child. In particular, this area extends further into the *tax basis of the assets* and the eventual *income tax consequences* from a subsequent sale.

Please note this conversation pertains to *income tax* and not the *estate tax*. Also, I will caution that my example is not by any means all-inclusive, but rather will be used to make a point that I feel can apply to a fairly large number of taxpayers.

Receiving noncash gifts

Assume that an elderly mother of two sons has cash of $500,000 and one thousand acres of farmland valued at $4,500,000. Their accountant has made her aware of the $5,000,000 estate tax exemption (for 2011), and the parent's goal is to avoid the estate being subject to the tax upon her death.

Furthermore, the mother wishes to begin drawing upon her assets and making gifts that do not trigger gift tax consequences, or annual gifts above $13,000. In short, she wishes to utilize a good tax avoidance strategy.

It has been my observation that in some cases the elderly make the mistake of giving acres of appreciated land to their children rather than giving cash. The reason I say this is a mistake is due to the cost-basis rules that come into play for the recipient of the gift.

For instance, assume in our example that all of the land was purchased forty years ago at $500 per acre, or $500,000 total. During this time, the market value of the land has skyrocketed to $4,500 per acre. Herein lies the potential income tax trap to the sons when land is gifted rather than cash.

If each son receives twenty acres of land before their mother's death, their cost basis under income tax rules must be assigned the same cost as that of the parent, or $500 per acre. If those twenty acres are later sold by each son at market value, or $90,000 for each son, there will be a gain of $80,000 each upon which to pay income tax at both the federal and state levels.

On the other hand, another twenty acres of that same farmland later inherited upon death of the mother will give a cost basis of $4,500 per acre to the beneficiaries, because income tax law dictates that cost basis be assigned market value as of the date of death, which in this case is assumed to remain at $4,500 per acre.

In this situation, if these inherited twenty acres were sold by each son, presumably at the market price of $90,000, the gain on the sale would be zero. Though identical in number of acres sold and sales price, the difference in these two sales examples (gifted versus inherited) would be approximately $20,000 in personal income tax.

Receiving cash gifts

So how could this tax trap have been avoided for the two sons? Simply, the mother could have instead given $13,000 cash to each son rather than the farmland. In this case, there will be no gain to worry about later, as in the case with the land that has high appreciation.

Incidentally, the argument just made for giving cash over land could also be given in the case of an elderly parent having stock with appreciated value. In this situation, inheriting the stock at death would give the beneficiaries the higher cost basis (market value), thereby yielding smaller gains and less tax when the investments were eventually sold.

Here in summary form is an analysis of the facts just mentioned:

Receiving land while mother living: - 1st case

Basis of land = same basis as mother	$500
times: number of acres	20
Equals tax basis of gifted land	10,000

Tax gain:

Proceeds at $4,500 per acre x 20 acres	90,000
Less tax basis from above calculation	(10,000)
Equals gain on sale	80,000

Receiving land upon mother's death: - 2nd case

Basis of land = fair market value at death	$4,500
times: number of acres	20
Equals tax basis of inherited land	90,000

Tax gain:

Proceeds at $4,500 per acre x 20 acres	90,000
Less tax basis from calculation	90,000
Equals gain on sale	0

I realize this is somewhat of a generic bit of advice that ignores some real-life issues such as family peace, financial trust, and fear of letting go of cash. No matter our age, we are all engrained to be prepared for a rainy day, especially the older generation, which is the model for us to follow. However, given the complexities of income tax law and the uncertainty of the estate tax exemption, it is good advice to keep in mind the cost-basis rules as one considers future estate tax planning.

Additionally, if gifting cash just isn't the comfortable choice for the donor, the strategy would then be to gift more recently purchased land or stocks, as the higher cost basis of these assets would carry over to the recipients, most likely meaning lesser gains later when the assets were sold.

Regardless of the choice, keep in mind to avoid, when practical, gifting farmland purchased cheaply years ago or stocks acquired at a low price that have substantially appreciated in value.

And finally, I would recommend one final piece of advice for the ones receiving gifts from parents who are trying to do the right thing for their children. Upon receiving any cash, one should set aside a portion of the funds just in case the parents' estate is eventually determined to be taxable. In our example, this could be due to farmland values continuing to appreciate, legislation lowering the exemption, or a combination of the two.

Taxable estates having a low percentage of cash might require assistance from the beneficiaries in order to meet estate tax obligations and prevent having to sell off inherited properties to raise the needed cash. This is a common reason why we see frequent estate sales of farmland in particular.

Again, simple discipline is a cure and prevention for so many financial ills. Just as it is better to receive than to give, financially speaking, it is even better to receive and prudently save some of our good fortunes.

Summary Points
- *When receiving a gift, there is never a current tax issue for the recipient.*
- *However, when eventually selling the gifted asset, there can be a range of income tax effects, such as having to report large taxable gains.*

- *Ideally, a donor should try to avoid giving assets that were purchased at a low cost, because recipients of gifts assume the same low tax cost, or basis, as the donor.*
- *For this reason, cash may be a better asset to gift because there are no eventual sales to trigger a taxable gain.*
- *Assuming cash is not a good option, gifting land or stock purchased more recently at a higher price is a good strategy, since the recipient will be assuming the same relatively higher basis as the donor.*
- *A larger tax basis will mean smaller gains for the donee when the asset is sold.*
- *In short, assets received at death are assigned a basis of fair market value; assets received by gift assume the basis of the donor.*

CHAPTER 13

What We Live In

WE NOW COME TO a topic that definitely has a common thread with most of the adult population, and that is housing. There is no other part of the US economy that has such a vital and rippling effect as the housing market. Banks, appliance manufacturers, metal extrusion companies, and concrete manufacturers are just a few of the industries that have such a huge reliance upon this part of the economy.

Just as we all must eat and have clothes on our backs, we also must have a roof over our heads, thus completing the third of life's three primary needs. Unlike food and clothing, housing can take on different forms of consumption such as renting a house, renting an apartment, or owning a home. The stage of housing in which one finds himself typically is related to maturity in life and income, as home ownership can require much time and financial commitment.

The purpose in discussing this topic is not to suggest what size house one should buy, or whether one should even purchase a house. Rather, the goal is to simplify the topic and suggest some guidelines to make this process less overwhelming.

Housing Affordability

I will in later chapters discuss what I feel are the two most serious factors hindering our abilities to accumulate net worth. However, I will here insert what I feel is the third most serious factor affecting the population, and that isn't *housing* itself, but *housing affordability*. There is a significant difference between the two.

Simply stated, only a very small percentage of the US population has the means to purchase a house without incurring debt. Even the most fiscally disciplined individuals and couples find it challenging to purchase that first home or eventual dream home with cash. This is where banks come into play with their ability to help us leverage the expensive purchase with long-term debt.

Being fiscally conservative, I still maintain that home ownership is the one area where we should treat ourselves and perhaps stretch ourselves a little financially. After all, this is an asset that in general appreciates or at least holds its value over time, as opposed to cars and trucks, which come and go every few years. Homes are a source of pride and establish family roots, whereas automobiles can be more of a source of personal glitter and short-term satisfaction.

Similar to preferences in music and food, the varieties of housing are equally as diverse. However, I do believe the following principles have merit to most people:

1. *Location should indeed be the main driver of housing choice. Some people may be guided by the desire to see a country sunset, whereas others may want their location to be based upon who their neighbors are. But regardless, no matter how beautiful the home, we need to want to be where we end up living.*
2. *Ideally, down payments should be at least 20 percent in order to protect against negative market swings impacting one's net worth. This can be a tough one to follow, especially if you find the ideal home but don't currently have the 20 percent. Also, down payments less than 20 percent generally require the borrower to pay for additional insurance in order to protect the lending institution in case of default.*

3. *If buyers don't feel comfortable taking the more expensive fifteen-year mortgage, as opposed to the thirty-year mortgage, every effort should be made as early as possible to make extra payments within the longer mortgage, even if just fifty dollars a month. A payoff in twenty years, if not sooner, should be the goal.*
4. *Housing should be a source of fulfillment and pride. Looking over one's shoulder at what your neighbors or coworkers have is about the worst thing you can do. Self-imposed peer pressure is what makes the 20 percent down payment objective so difficult to achieve, as we tend to get caught up in the rat race of looking for bigger and better to keep up with the Joneses.*
5. *Each change in home ownership requires expensive fees and market risks. Individuals should have a long-range plan for what stage in their life they would like to achieve their dream home. Unless one just enjoys moving every few years for something new, a long-range plan can help minimize costly ownership changes.*
6. *In general, home ownership is the best choice for the long term, giving security of staying in one place as well as the potential for financial appreciation. However, during times of economic uncertainties, renting can be a very attractive source of housing for the short to medium term. Location becomes the main challenge with this option, but, financially, renting relieves so much pressure from large upfront obligations. Home ownership is, therefore, not always the cure-all answer for everyone.*
7. *Refer again to item 4. This point definitely is worthy of being repeated.*

No doubt many things could be added in the way of more specific advice, such as using home inspectors, or how to look for the best mortgage rates. However, our focus here is really on the bigger picture, and I am very much swayed by what happened in 2008 in the real estate market. Even now, four years later, I often read of statistics which indicate that nearly 50 percent of Americans have a negative net worth in their housing, meaning simply that the house is worth less than what is owed to the bank.

Personally, I find it very disturbing that such a solid long-term investment as housing can be strapping down so many people in the way of mobility, in particular. I am sure there are many people who would like to move to another neighborhood or move closer to a new job but simply cannot because they have little or no equity, or even negative equity in the existing home. The sad part about this feeling is that it takes away a certain degree of hope, which in my opinion is the inner fabric of chasing the American dream. This is why I am so headstrong on the belief that one should save for a 20 percent down payment.

Effectively, this gives the homeowner an earned equity cushion of being able to absorb an immediate crash in real estate value and still be able to have positive equity in the investment. Also, any down payment less than 20 percent generally requires private mortgage insurance, or PMI, which protects the lending institution in cases when a forced sale brings in sales proceeds less than the debt owed. Being passed to the borrower, the PMI effectively becomes an additional cost of borrowing until sufficient equity is built.

POWER OF THE EXTRA PAYMENT

In addition to the goal of 20 percent down, homeowners should choose the fifteen-year mortgage if practical. These two objectives would help so many of us in the long term. But, unfortunately, Americans generally prefer to take shortcuts that favor increased spending now and less money being set aside for savings.

For instance, we prefer to buy the largest and most expensive house we can, but we want to finance it as cheaply as possible. Notice the flaw in that wish. On the one hand is a home with a very expensive price, but on the other hand we are asking to pay for it with as small payments as we can. So what gives? The only way this can be reconciled is payment terms extending to the maximum, or generally thirty years. And, unfortunately, the further out in time the higher the interest rate charged by the banks.

By way of example, a 5.5 percent loan of $200,000 financed over thirty years, with 20 percent down, would require a monthly payment of $908. To show the effect of good financial discipline, the following extra payments made each month would yield these reductions in lives of the loans:

Monthly Extra Payment	Gives a Reduction in Years of	(With Extra) Total Principal and Interest	(With No Extra) Total Principal and Interest	Extra Payment Savings
$50	3.6	343,833	367,046	23,213
100	6.3	326,403	367,046	40,643
200	10.3	302,706	367,046	64,340

Note the effect of making the additional $200 per month. In total, the interest payments are reduced by over $64,000, with the term of the loan effectively becoming twenty years. Unfortunately, I don't think most people truly appreciate the impact of having ten years removed from servicing a mortgage.

Very simply, this means a thirty-year-old couple buying a house now would be mortgage free at age fifty rather than sixty. Yes, sacrifices must be made to achieve the end result, but the thought of saving $64,000 in interest that could be spent elsewhere, on college education or just something fun and rewarding, is to me an exciting challenge worth pursuing.

With interest rates at all-time lows, this is an extremely favorable time for individuals to pursue the American dream, albeit in a time of great uncertainty. However, with commonsense savings to achieve the 20 percent down payment plus financial discipline to pay down a mortgage early, home ownership can be a great way to achieve positive net worth using long-term debt.

Again, going back to our example, it would not be unrealistic at all to assume the $200,000 home would appreciate to $300,000 in a twenty-year span. Under this assumption, the $100,000 appreciation would nearly negate all of the interest paid of $102,706 under the extra $200 per month scenario.

Also, if you happen to be living in your American dream, there are still rewards that can be reaped in today's favorable mortgage market. Remarkably, a rate of 3 percent can be locked in today on a fifteen-year mortgage. Assuming you have a rate of 4.5 percent or higher, whether on a fifteen- or thirty-year loan, one can quickly recover the refinancing costs from the reduced interest costs on a new 3 percent loan. For every 1 percent rate reduction on a $100,000 mortgage, for example, the savings would be $1,000 annually. Don't turn your back on such a free pay raise.

In short, housing can be a worthy and fulfilling investment to pursue, but remember the ultimate attainment of that goal will be influenced greatly by one's housing affordability. That is, a healthy level of down payment combined with strong payment discipline after the purchase can accelerate a nice accumulation of net worth within a household.

Conversely, as evidenced by today's real estate market, excess wants and the extension of financing terms to maximum lengths can actually pull a family's net worth position in the opposite direction. Most of us have to make the financial sacrifice. The only question is when in our lives we choose to do so.

Summary Points
- *Housing can be one of the best investments you ever make, giving both personal enjoyment as well as financial equity.*
- *Similar to buying a car, one's purchase of a home shouldn't be guided by the maximum monthly payment that one can afford over a thirty-year loan.*
- *Ideally, a mortgage should be fifteen years, financed with at least a 20 percent down payment.*

CHAPTER 13 EXERCISE

Evaluate your current mortgage by inserting the following details:

Original purchase price of house	_____
Date of purchase	_____
Original debt on house	_____
Any 2nd mortgage added?	_____
Total mortgage owed today	_____
Term (15, 30 yr)	_____
Interest rate	_____
Adjustable, or fixed rate	_____
Monthly payment	_____

Consider the following money-saving strategies:
If you have extra money and don't know where to invest, simply pay extra on your mortgage. Whatever rate you are paying will effectively become what you earn by making the extra payments.

If your existing rate is 1.5 percent or greater than market, refinance and realize a pay increase.

If your mortgage is an adjustable rate, refinance and lock in current attractive rates rather than watching them eventually increase.

Calculate the annual payments you are making on your mortgage and let that be motivation to make extra payments. At an earlier payoff, you will effectively enjoy a pay raise equal to your prior annual mortgage commitment.

CHAPTER 14

Money on Wheels

WE NOW COME TO a discussion of one of the two previously mentioned major deterrents to financial health for most Americans, and that is the consumption of automobiles. I firmly believe this is one area of personal finance that is the most neglected, yet has potentially the most to offer in the way of increased net worth.

MY PERSONAL EXPERIENCE
Before I begin this topic, I will be the first to confess that I've endured some battle scars along the way in regard to the purchase of an automobile. Being a young adult in the mid-1980s, I was still in that time frame when going to the automobile dealer alone was an invitation to get gouged by slick dealers. In fact, I am humble enough to admit that at age twenty-two I was suckered into that timeless trick of giving the salesman a little cash to let him pass along to his "manager" that I was making a serious offer. That is one experience from which I definitely ate a healthy piece of humble pie.

However, being able to still remember that salesman's name to this day shows the value of getting burned once, and vowing to never let it happen again. Thinking about it now still irks me, and if I ever meet that salesman again I will sarcastically give him another wad of cash to thank him for the lesson he gave me back in 1987.

Nowadays, the Internet has empowered so many people with financial knowledge of automobiles that it has made new car buying an extremely tough market for dealers. Don't get me wrong. I firmly believe that car dealers still make their share of profits. However, the ability to comparison shop for new automobiles in particular has made it more of a buyer's market than ever before.

In turn, I believe the hazy dickering of numbers has moved more to the used auto market, where it is harder for buyers to get a firm grasp of the cost numbers. Nonetheless, it is still a better time to shop now than it was for me at the gullible age of twenty-two.

As stated early in the book, cars are in today's world Maslow-type assets that we rely upon greatly to get to work and make a living. Most of the US population could not make it without them. Also, with so many couples being two-wage earners, it is a fairly common standard for the typical US family to have at least two automobiles. This will be the assumption that I use as we get into the discussion of automobile consumption.

No matter how shiny and well maintained you choose to keep your car, inevitably it will end up in a scrap yard at some point in time. You can make the same argument for a house, I suppose, but fifty or sixty years worth of utility from a house pretty much takes care of your needs for your adult life. On the other hand, adults who live a normal life will go through perhaps a dozen or two car "life cycles," which in my definition is simply the time span in years between the purchase and eventual disposition of a car.

Vehicle use is really no different than our everyday needs to have food and clothing. Just as I sit down to eat three meals a day, which pulls food out of the refrigerator, the use of my truck is very similar in that each use essentially takes it toward its eventual death. Therefore, my discussion of this very important topic is going to be in terms of *vehicle consumption*, which in turn will equate to *financial cost*.

CAR SHOPPING STRATEGY

First of all, I wish to stress three very important points that I believe should be followed when looking to purchase an automobile, especially one that is new. For one, try to make a determination before you walk into a showroom as to what you wish to purchase. I really don't think this is an issue for most of us due to the advertising that we see. As a result, most of us know pretty much what we want. But when you do walk into the showroom, let it be known what you want, that you are going to make a decision in a day or two, and that at least one other dealer is going to get the same opportunity. All of these collectively let the dealer know that you mean business and that you are not there to waste time.

Second, if the dealer begins to stammer and ask you the monthly payment you can afford, interrupt before he or she finishes the question and let him or her know that financing is no issue. You are there only to see if the product you want is available and to determine the purchase price of the automobile. Ideally, one should have a tentative financing plan established before walking into the dealer's doors, whether it be all cash, a loan through a credit union, or a loan through one's 401(k) plan.

Personally, if I am asked the monthly payment question, that salesman automatically gets a mark against him or her and the dealership. The final choice of financing should be one of the last steps in purchasing a vehicle. But if you answer this question with a payment figure, you are essentially giving the dealership the upper hand in price negotiation, as the salesman can in turn adjust the interest rate, payment period, and trade-in allowance to blur the purchase and make you feel like you are getting a good deal. It is all a smoke and mirrors routine, so my advice is to focus on determining the purchase price and refuse to answer monthly payment questions.

If you are close to my age group, perhaps you remember the amazing deals of zero percent financing that started to appear in 1986. Do you think the reason for this is that the automakers suddenly woke up one day and decided to be extra nice? Believe it or not, Ronald Reagan had a large influence in this. Prior to this time, all personal interest was tax deductible. The Tax Reform Act of 1986 disallowed all personal interest except mortgage and home equity, thus removing a strong marketing point of selling cars under financing plans.

Zero percent plans, therefore, began to be common. However, to get the zero percent you paid a price higher than if you financed yourself or paid in cash. Again, if something seems too good to be true, then it probably is. This is a classic case in point.

Third, do not allow a salesman to talk you into an extended warranty that you had no intention of buying. I respect those who feel that warranties are good, perhaps from the feeling of security they give. However, I personally have to question anyone who is selling me a $30,000 product that has just been glorified in the sales pitch, asking me if I would be interested in taking out maintenance insurance. What kind of look would I get if I offered an extended warranty to a prospective buyer of my new house? I really don't see any difference.

My caution to you is simply this: after feeling like you earned a good deal on the car purchase, avoid the last line of temptations that will come your way as you sit down with the salesman and are asked about extended warranties, scotch-guard protection, and all such extra add-ons.

Without meaning to sound like the skeptic that I'm not, dealerships do not offer these extras because they are nice guys. Rather, these are items which, if chosen, can turn a thin-margin sale into a decent profit for the dealership. I am as convinced of that as I am that politicians don't always look out for the good of the voting public.

Vehicle consumption

Stepping aside from the purchase and financing details, I now wish to cover what I think is the essence of vehicles and their impact upon net worth, and that is vehicle consumption. In very simple terms, we all effectively pay annual rent to drive our automobiles. For example, an individual who purchases a car in year 1 for $30,000, keeps it for five years, and then trades it in, receiving a $10,000 trade-in allowance at the end of year 5, has these costs of car ownership:

Initial purchase price at beginning of year 1	$ 30,000
Less trade-in allowance at end of year 5	(10,000)
Equals total net cost of vehicle	20,000
Annual cost over 5 years	4,000

Assuming the same facts for a couple with two cars, the annual cost would be $8,000. For sake of simplicity, this analysis excludes maintenance, repairs, and insurance, as these are all costs that cannot be avoided and are really outside of the topic at hand. Furthermore, interest costs are excluded as well, as the focus here is on the actual purchase price of the vehicles. Again, our goal is simplicity.

Continuing the example for a married couple, assume at the beginning of year 6 they purchase two cars for $35,000 each. Again, husband and wife choose to keep the vehicles five years, at which time each of the vehicles yield a trade-in allowance of $10,000. Here would be the annual costs for each of these vehicles:

Initial purchase price at beginning of year 6	$35,000
Less trade-in allowance at end of year 10	(10,000)
Equals total net cost of vehicle	25,000
Annual cost over 5 years – one vehicle	5,000
Annual cost over 5 years – two vehicles	10,000

At this point, I think you get the idea as to how to calculate the effective financial cost of vehicle consumption. Very simply, the cost is influenced greatly by our taste in vehicles, and, furthermore, by the length of time we choose to keep the vehicle. Many will contend that turning vehicles over quicker will pay off by keeping newer vehicles that require less maintenance. However, I maintain that any reduction in maintenance costs achieved will be offset by higher insurance and property taxes.

Personally, I have in general chosen $2,500 to $3,000 to be the annual cost per vehicle that I have allowed myself to pay over my adult life. So this means for two vehicles, $5,000 to $6,000 has been the effective annual cost for my household. By no means would I say this has been easy to achieve because, like most people, I enjoy driving something new. However, I have informally chosen a strategy to keep a vehicle for eight years before I allow myself to trade.

I must confess my eight-year plan has no more financial substance than simply being rooted in common sense. If nothing else, staying out of the dealer showroom as long as you can reduces the number of times one must be exposed to the risk of trade-ins or selling old vehicles. Unless one just relishes the challenge of negotiating, staying away from automobile transactions seems to me a winning proposition.

Furthermore, keeping a vehicle eight years, particularly one bought new, should not be viewed with a negative connotation. After all, even driving a high rate of 20,000 miles per year means the vehicle would have 160,000 miles at the end of eight years. By today's standards, this doesn't suggest the car is ready for the grave. A generation ago perhaps, but today we have better products to drive, which give us longer usefulness.

Also, as far as financing is concerned, vehicle loans are commonly set up on four-year terms. Doing simple math, a family owning two vehicles financed with four-year loans will, on average, always have loan payments if the family's consumption pattern is anything less than eight years. In my opinion, opportunities to increase net worth are greatly enhanced during periods when families are relieved of making vehicle loan payments.

However, some people seem resigned to the fact that car payments are simply a way of life and cannot be avoided. I firmly deny that way of thinking and instead maintain that *costs of vehicle consumption* (not *payments*) cannot be avoided, just as costs of nourishing our bodies cannot be avoided. However, through prudence, patience, and down payment discipline, the timing of payments can be such that a family doesn't have to be continually tied to vehicle debt.

Types of Car Buyers

I will now interject a healthier degree of my personal opinion and suggest three categories that describe consumers of vehicles. The first type, who I will call the *marathon runner,* is one who purchases and keeps vehicles for an average of eight or more years. The second type, the *five-mile runner,* is one who gets the itch to buy a little quicker and falls between the four- and eight-year range. The third type, the *hundred yard sprinter,* being the itchiest of them all, is the one who will find a way to buy and trade every two or three years.

How do you know the group to which you belong? Personally, I consider myself to be the marathon runner, mainly because of my strong feeling as to how I view vehicles as a deterrent to long-term financial health. However, a quick exercise that we can easily do puts me on the borderline with being the five-mile runner.

Very simply, go back in time and add up all car and truck purchases you have made after your first purchase (don't include the first one), and divide that total into the number of years that have passed since. In my case, my first purchase was in 1987. Since then, we have purchased six automobiles in a span of twenty-five years.

Using my equation, this would be twenty-five years divided by six, giving an answer of just over 4. If I was single during these years, this would mean that I had on average kept my vehicles for a period of four years. However, giving effect to being married and there being two of us, I need to multiply by two, giving a value of 8. In other words, on average my wife and I have held each of our six vehicles for an average of eight years.

Coming up on age forty-eight, if I had to pick a financial strategy that has proven to be my friend, this would be one of our top two or three accomplishments. Very simply, through a gradual process we have been able to accumulate new worth by effectively *managing* the cost of vehicles.

Notice I didn't say we have *avoided* the costs. Rather, it has been an unspectacular effort of simply spreading the costs of car ownership over time. I probably enjoy the smell of a new car as much as anyone, but I have always had that little guy on my shoulder reminding me that in the long-run, the pursuit of new wheels can be a money pit because of the depreciation of the asset.

As for the five-mile runner group, I would recommend simply adding some time discipline to ownership. If you typically keep a car for the length of the loan, say four years, then try adding one year before going back to the dealer. As I write this, I smile and tell myself repeatedly that we all are different creatures of likes and dislikes, and that giving this advice to some is like telling a fish not to swim. However, if just a small degree of sacrifice can be made, the savings can be significant.

Lastly, going to the group of hundred yard sprinters, I again wish to show my practical side of giving advice and suggest leasing to be a viable strategy. Personally, I am about as much "antilease" as you can get, as I maintain that automobile dealers wouldn't push leases if they weren't profitable for their business.

However, I definitely think leases offer value to those consumers who just can't seem to stay away from the lure of a new car. For example, most leases are at least for terms of four years. If you are one who has a pattern of buying every two to three years, a lease term of four years, ironically, will provide you with a measure of time discipline. Furthermore, leasing allows one to avoid market risks associated with trading or selling an older vehicle.

COMPARATIVE COSTS BETWEEN BUYER TYPES

Having said all of that, I will always maintain car ownership to be the best option over the long run to most effectively manage the inherent costs of personal transportation. Without going into needless details, I choose to leave this topic with a simple illustration.

I have chosen to use two examples of married couples over a fifty-year span. Couple A is a consistent four-year purchaser of vehicles, meaning on average they are going to the dealership every two years to buy a car for either spouse. On the other hand, couple B chooses to hang on to their vehicles for eight years, thus averaging a purchase of every four years between the two spouses. I have assumed trading after four years will yield a 40 percent trade allowance, and waiting until eight years will give a lower allowance of 20 percent. Also, I have assumed car costs of $25,000 in the early years and $45,000 in the late years.

In brief, choosing the eight-year pattern of consumption would, over fifty years, leave couple B with $185,000 of additional net worth over that of couple A. Before naysayers shoot me down and suggest that I didn't factor in the increased cost of maintenance for couple B, I would again state in return that lower property taxes and insurance costs would most likely offset this concern, on average.

Also, my analysis assumes all purchases are cash only, thus somewhat unrealistic and highly conservative. If interest payments were included, I suspect the total difference in cash payouts would be in the neighborhood of a quarter of a million dollars. The supporting calculations of the $185,000 principal savings are as follows:

Couple A – keep a car four years:

Years	Cost of vehicle	Trade-in allow. = 40%	Net cost	Annual cost for each car	Annual cost for two cars	Total cost 4-yr. life
1-4	25,000	(10,000)	15,000	3,750	7,500	30,000
5-8	25,000	(10,000)	15,000	3,750	7,500	30,000
9-12	30,000	(12,000)	18,000	4,500	9,000	36,000
13-16	30,000	(12,000)	18,000	4,500	9,000	36,000
17-20	35,000	(14,000)	21,000	5,250	10,500	42,000
21-24	35,000	(14,000)	21,000	5,250	10,500	42,000
25-28	40,000	(16,000)	24,000	6,000	12,000	48,000
29-32	40,000	(16,000)	24,000	6,000	12,000	48,000
33-36	45,000	(18,000)	27,000	6,750	13,500	54,000
37-40	45,000	(18,000)	27,000	6,750	13,500	54,000
41-44	45,000	(18,000)	27,000	6,750	13,500	54,000
45-48	45,000	(18,000)	27,000	6,750	13,500	54,000
49-50	45,000	(18,000)	27,000	6,750	13,500	27,000

Total vehicle costs   555,000

Average cost per year of vehicle consumption   11,100

Couple B– keep a car eight years:

Years	Cost of vehicle	Trade-in allow. = 20%	Net cost	Annual cost for each car	Annual cost for two cars	Total cost 8-yr. life
1-8	25,000	(5,000)	20,000	2,500	5,000	40,000
9-16	30,000	(6,000)	24,000	3,000	6,000	48,000
17-24	35,000	(7,000)	28,000	3,500	7,000	56,000
25-32	40,000	(8,000)	32,000	4,000	8,000	64,000
33-40	45,000	(9,000)	36,000	4,500	9,000	72,000
41-48	45,000	(9,000)	36,000	4,500	9,000	72,000
49-50	45,000	(9,000)	36,000	4,500	9,000	18,000

Total vehicle costs   370,000

Average cost per year   7,400
vehicle consumption

In summary, I suggest to you that simply turning on the television and watching the automobile advertisements is all the proof we need to confirm the impact of this industry. Like nearly every other business, the success of the automobile industry depends in large part upon the individual consumers and their patterns of consumption.

Being a firm believer in economic winners and losers, I maintain that excess consumption in the car market has fattened the wallets of the automakers while taking away from the long-term wealth of the general population. If cars weren't depreciating assets, I wouldn't dare make that statement. Remember that list of seven vehicles I have purchased? Only two are in my driveway, while the other five have gone elsewhere and are nowhere to be found on my list of assets.

Remember the eight-year rule, and allow it to at least be a consideration for your purchasing and financing decisions. If you truly want freedom from the burden of car payments, a modest amount of discipline will take you a long way toward that end.

Summary Points
- *Vehicle purchases are one of the biggest negative factors that pull down a family's accumulation of net worth.*

- *Prestige and status are strong personal elements that can go against making sound financial decisions when purchasing a car.*
- *Vehicle consumption is the annual financial cost of owning a vehicle; ideally, ownership for at least eight years will help reduce vehicle consumption costs.*

Chapter 14 Exercise

Evaluate your personal vehicle consumption by completing the following history of your purchases:

				[A]	[B]	= [A] / [B]
Auto	Date purchased	Cost	Minus Trade-in from old auto	Net Cost	# years owned	Vehicle Consumption
___	___	___	___	___	___	___
___	___	___	___	___	___	___
___	___	___	___	___	___	___
___	___	___	___	___	___	___
___	___	___	___	___	___	___

This evaluation isn't meant to be an exact science, but rather an exercise to get you thinking in terms of annual costs of car ownership. This will be the calculation made in the far-right-hand column. Typically, as the number of years of ownership increases, the annual vehicle consumption will decrease.

In column B, the number of years owned among vehicles will give you a self-analysis of holding patterns of your vehicles among the three types:

1. *The marathon runner—eight years or more*
2. *The five-mile runner—four to eight years*
3. *The hundred yard sprinter—less than four years*

In summary, the lesson to be learned in this chapter is that net worth can be significantly increased over one's lifetime by smarter choices in the holding period for automobiles. That is, the fewer times one must enter the dealership, the better off one should be financially.

CHAPTER 15

How to Earn a 17.5 Percent Return

BEING INVOLVED IN THE area of tax, I have often been asked over the past several years, in particular, my recommendations for investing. With stock market uncertainty and interest rates at historic lows, individuals having excess funds have simply been bewildered as to where to invest. Unfortunately, there no longer seems to be a good answer to give as money market and certificate of deposit rates have been less than 0.5 percent.

Though I find it flattering that tax clients value my financial opinion, I also realize that I truly do not have the expertise to make such recommendations, nor do I wish to stick my neck out to recommend something and then be proven wrong by someone else's financial loss.

Unfortunately, a sure winner of a plan that I do have doesn't fit the profile of the typical client who usually asks me these investment questions. This client is commonly over age sixty, retired, and has no debt. Also, this client has no real desire to aggressively enter the stock market and take advantage of recent lows in market prices, and for that I find no fault. Being sixty and over, one wishes instead to find something relatively safe, thus contributing to the dilemma of finding decent investments during times of historically low rates.

Before discussing a way to earn a 17.5 percent return, I wish to first discuss what I think is the second of the two major factors keeping Americans from achieving long-term financial wealth, and that is the credit card. Pure and simple, the credit card has given both the best of times to many Americans, and the worst of times.

To those who have enjoyed the good times, the credit card has offered ease of transactions, particularly when out of town and in foreign countries, as well as the ability to purchase over the Internet. To those who have been impacted negatively, the credit card has, ironically, affected these individuals due to the same reasons. The common thread applicable to both groups is again financial discipline, with the former group having such and the latter group lacking it.

My personal view of the credit card

Being a credit card customer for over twenty years, I have slowly come to the conclusion that the inherent bad that many of us hear regarding credit cards does not necessarily have to be true. Generally speaking, my generation of late baby boomers has been the first to fully embrace frequent use of the credit card. The generation of my parents, what I would refer to as the early baby boomers, has tended to use the credit card more cautiously and view it as an easy invitation to reckless spending. Being the predictable accountant I am, my financial behavior has settled somewhere in the middle.

Whether we as consumers care to admit it, we are all purchasers of goods whose price is reflective of the underlying cost of bad credit in the economy. That is, if we are charged $100 for a coat, you can bet that perhaps $1 to $2 of that asking price will be collected to compensate the retailer for bad consumers. So effectively, the good-paying customers subsidize those who either can't pay their debts or refuse to pay.

This same principle, unfortunately, applies for other areas of negative behavior. For instance, those who steal merchandise collectively account for a financial cost to society, just as the actions of arsonists drive up the cost of doing business and mean higher insurance premiums. Furthermore, the cost of deterring and catching such negative behavior shows up in the form of added police protection, which in turn requires more tax revenues, and thus more costs passed on to the eventual consumer. We could go on and on with such negative examples.

What I wish to bring into focus now is my view of how the credit card actually rewards those consumers having good financial discipline. I have two credit cards, one of which pays back a 1 percent bonus for all purchases, while the other gives a 5 percent bonus toward the purchase of a new GM vehicle. Assuming I use both cards equally, I am effectively able to reduce my cost of purchases by an average of 3 percent. However, my basis for that statement can only be supported by paying off the credit card balances each month. If that assumption isn't followed, then all my positive comments suddenly become way off base.

To continue my point, if I choose instead to use checks or cash to pay for these same goods and services, I would be foregoing the 3 percent paybacks and choosing instead to pay full asking price and subsidize the costs of bad debts of others. Personally, I choose to use my credit cards to pay for as many items as possible, both for convenience and to leverage the 1 percent and 5 percent paybacks.

For items that are unavoidable purchases, I consider the choice of using a credit card to be a no-brainer. For instance, I must have automobile and housing insurance, gasoline, groceries, and medical services. Collectively, these can easily come to $25,000 per year. At a 3 percent average rebate, that is $750 going into my pocket versus paying with checks and cash.

Furthermore, I must admit that my annual credit card purchases come to more than the $25,000 in my example. Therefore, you can easily assume that on a personal basis I choose to use credit cards for dining, clothing, and other items that are more discretionary in nature.

I will be the first to acknowledge that at times the swiping of the card makes things so easy, especially on vacation or during the holiday shopping spree. I do not dare pretend to come across as one who has never been surprised by the credit card balance owing on the next month's statement. However, the balance always gets paid in full, thus requiring my wife and me to at least be held accountable for those purchases made in the prior month.

To this point, it should be quite clear that I have shown my bias toward the use of credit cards in my own personal life. I will be the first to acknowledge my good fortune of my wife and I both having good jobs and not having outrageous medical or college tuition bills to pay. If negative circumstances came our way, no doubt the use of credit cards for our discretionary purchases would come under much more scrutiny. However, I still maintain that I would be a user of the credit card, albeit on a more limited basis.

GROUPS OF CREDIT CARD USERS

At this point, I would like to summarize three general groups of individuals who have characteristics that either do or do not lend themselves to compatibility with credit card usage. Perhaps my way of thinking is too simplistic, but I feel the merits of simplicity are greater than benefits from considering countless scenarios. The three groups I have chosen to label are as follows:

1. *Disciplined users who pay the monthly balance*
2. *Users who finance the balance, but always make some payment*
3. *Undisciplined users who occasionally make the minimum payment*

A *first group* user is one who will come out ahead through purchasing with the credit card and receiving the incentives and rebates. The discounts effectively reward the prudent credit card user for paying balances in full and on time. As an example, I have so far been able to reduce the purchase price of two automobiles by $5,000 through the use of my GM account balances.

To counter any skeptics, I have used these credits in both instances when the final sales price was determined, thus avoiding any smoke and mirrors shifting of the numbers. In short, the choice of discipline in paying off balances has rewarded me with genuine financial returns.

Furthermore, the characteristics of this group are such that given a bad month when credit purchases prove to be far above that expected, the individual will find every way possible to pay down the debt the next month, even if it means tapping into a savings account or canceling a planned purchase. In other words, this group knows the downfall of allowing the credit balance to turn into 18 percent debt and reacts accordingly.

Skipping to the *third group* user, this is the individual who views a credit card as a one-month license to shop. Quite simply, it is extremely difficult for this person to handle the responsibilities of a credit card. When these users see something they like, they swipe. Something else comes along that glitters, and they swipe again. In a matter of days, they find a way to reach the maximum limit without thinking of the payments to come later.

When the monthly bill is received, this person tends to look at the minimum payment due and pays accordingly. For example, if $5,000 of purchases were incurred, requiring a minimum payment of $200, the buyer is immediately swept into a loan financed at 18 percent. Unfortunately, at such an interest rate, the $200 minimum payment for the first month can only be applied to $125 of debt, as the interest for the month is $75. Therefore, assuming the best case of no credit card use the next month, the individual will now be facing a debt of $4,875. If the $200 minimum payment is made each month thereafter, it will take thirty-three months to pay this entire debt.

The example above naively assumes the individual in this group will continue making the $200 minimum payment and will not make any more purchases during the thirty-three-month period. Typically however, such an individual will only occasionally make the minimum payment, perhaps only after repeated attempts by the credit card company to collect. Many times, the individual's credit line will be taken away, and worst case, the credit card company may end up writing off the remaining debt owed by the customer.

In my opinion, this type of individual gains at the expense of the credit card company, as purchases are made that never end up being paid in full. However, keep in mind the gain is short term in nature, as future sources of credit may become hard to obtain from lending institutions and other credit card companies.

Lastly, the *second group* user of the three mentioned is the individual who frequently uses credit cards and has the means and discipline to consistently make the minimum payment due each month. Ironically, it is this person who is the bread and butter for the credit card companies.

The individual in the second group is the one consistently making payments on 18 percent loans, thus helping to fund the rebates given to the group one purchasers and subsidizing the bad debt losses generated by the group three purchasers. In business, there are winners and losers within each transaction. In this case, the losers are clearly the loyal credit card customers making payments on 18 percent loans.

Passive Investing

From my years of tax preparation, I have been able to observe quite a variety of financial behaviors, both from a savings and spending standpoint. While not privy to as much of the spending details, I have been around long enough to put together logical conclusions about why an individual making significant income generates only a modest level of interest and dividends. For instance, it is fairly common to observe one who sets aside a modest amount of money in a credit union, drawing perhaps 0.5 percent in today's market.

Furthermore, one who is a fairly disciplined credit union saver may also fall under the description of the second group of credit card users. Specifically, I find many people put certain items on "financial cruise" and never change, such as the automatic withdrawal into a credit union (a positive behavior) or the monthly payment of the minimum owed on a credit card (a negative behavior).

Getting caught up in the daily grind of life in general, I will be the first to admit it is very easy to keep doing the same things without putting thought into the financial implications. Similar to dust collecting in a room, we all are guilty of letting the minor details of finances slowly build into a much larger negative trend over time.

Without making this complex, I maintain that some group-two credit card users have the potential to easily generate 17.5 percent annual returns. First of all, my advice does not require *active investing*, which is the placement of funds with either stockbrokers or banks in hopes of achieving dividends, capital gains, or interest income. Therefore, one doesn't have to call a broker, visit a bank, or contact a financial website. Rather, one merely has to do what I refer to as *passive investing*, which is simply the paying down of debt.

Let me use what I feel is a fairly typical scenario for many Americans. Assume a person has a job making $50,000 a year and sets aside 3 percent of his paycheck, or $1,500, into a local credit union paying 0.5 percent interest. Additionally, this person is a user of just one credit card and always pays at least the minimum due each month. With a credit limit of $10,000, he generally feels comfortable to keep the balance owed at $5,000, rarely allowing it to go much higher.

Herein lies a blind spot of opportunity that many are missing. On the one hand, the $1,500 set aside in the credit union during the year will yield just over $4 in interest income. While this seems the prudent thing to do, consider the impact of taking the same $1,500, bypassing the credit union, and paying down an extra $125 per month on the credit card balance. Though interest earnings won't be reported on an IRS tax statement, the true effect will be realized through an increase in net worth as follows:

Case 1 – Assume $5,000 of credit card debt is maintained each month and $125 is invested with the credit union:

Interest expense at 18% would be	$900
Less interest income at 0.5% on the $125/month	(4)
Excess of interest expense over interest income	896

Case 2 – Assume $125 extra is applied to the credit card balance each month and nothing is invested with the credit union:

Interest expense at 18% would be	$754
Less interest income (nothing put in credit union)	0
Excess of interest expense over interest income	754

Fields of Green

Though not a lot of money, the difference in net cost between the two strategies is $142, or $896 minus $754. However, on the extra payment principal of $125 per month (or the $1,500 annual amount), this equates to an effective return of around 17.5 percent. In simple math, this is the 18 percent savings achieved through paying down debt less the 0.5 percent interest income that was foregone in order to make better use of the $1,500 previously deposited in the credit union.

A very simple lesson to learn from this is that a reduction of interest expense is just as important to financial well-being as any increase in interest income. With credit card debt at 18 percent, it borders on recklessness to have excess money sitting around in a money market yielding practically zero returns.

If a person feels the need to maintain a savings account for security reasons, I can appreciate that and do understand the anxiety of sacrificing excess cash in efforts to reduce debt. However, if this is the case, I strongly recommend leveraging a home equity loan to pay off the credit card debt, thus replacing 18 percent debt with perhaps 5 percent. The results won't be quite as positive, but nonetheless will generate an easy 13 percent return. Try finding that kind of return in today's market.

Debt in itself is not a bad thing, if chosen in the right manner. Residential and home equity loans are great examples that yield additional benefits in the way of tax deductions. If you're unsure of the return, simply look at your loan agreement. The interest rate you are being charged will become the actual return you will realize on making any extra payments. It's a different way of thinking, but in reality it boils down to the essence of net worth.

In short, credit card financing isn't the answer to effective saving, any more than putting excess money into vehicle consumption. Again, I believe these two things will forever be the downfall of so many Americans, as I currently see and read proof each and every day. It is my sincere wish that you now look at 18 percent financing as an opportunity rather than the black hole of financing. In my predictable fashion, it just takes time, discipline, and a dedicated change in financial behavior.

Summary Points
- *Group one credit card users benefit the most by receiving bonus perks and avoiding interest charges through paying off the balance each month.*
- *Group three card users benefit the next most by purchasing goods and oftentimes never paying the balance owed.*
- *Group two cards users are most negatively impacted by consistently paying on 18 percent credit card debt.*

Chapter 15 Exercise

Go back to the exercise in chapter 3 and insert the following asset and liability balances that were entered there:

Assets - Savings and checking account balances _____
Assets – Certificates of deposits _____
Liabilities – Credit card balances _____

Ideally, the credit card balances should be such that they are being paid off in full each month, meaning you are a group one credit card user. If not, it is safe to assume the credit card debt is carrying an interest rate of at least 18 percent.

Next, evaluate if the total of your assets above are as much as your credit card debt balances. If so, you are most likely missing a great opportunity to impact your net worth by paying off the credit card balance being financed. The calculation is as follows:

Credit card interest rate _____
Less average rate of earnings on savings _____
Equals: passive investment rate _____
    that could be realized

The passive investment rate times the credit card balance will give you the annual maximum increase in net worth that can be realized by simply taking the low-earning assets and putting them to better use through reduction of debt with an extremely high interest rate.

Some people have a difficult time parting with any savings, perhaps fearing for a rainy day use. However, keeping in mind the net worth concept, one must remember that liabilities are just as important of a factor in wealth as are the assets. It becomes a task of identifying the major negative-impact liabilities and removing them through the use of corresponding low positive-impact assets.

CHAPTER 16

Don't Fall in Love with These Two Things

THROUGHOUT A FEW CHAPTERS we have discussed how best to manage certain costs of living over time, focusing on how to extend the useful lives of more expensive items such as automobiles, in particular. Using simple math, the strategy has been to save money over the long term by making the annual cost less expensive through holding the asset longer. This way of thinking revolves more around consumer spending and modifying our behavior in a more disciplined way.

I wish now to think more on the supply side of consumer behavior, or more simply, one's income. It is well known that Americans in particular do not do the best job of taking after-tax pay and making ends meet. Quite simply, if after-tax pay is less than what we spend, we either must pull money out of savings, if any, or incur debt to finance the difference. When our pay is more than our personal spending, we can either add to savings or reduce debt.

It has been my general observation that many people choose to live their financial lives in much the same way as going to car showrooms and telling the salesmen what monthly payment they can afford. In other words, the goal is pretty much to spend every dollar of after-tax pay that is available. If it's there, it will be spent.

Too many rationalize this way of thinking by pointing to their Social Security and 401(k) plans that are being funded toward retirement. But as discussed earlier, this can be dangerous, especially if insufficient money has been set aside, or if funds have been taken out of the 401(k) prematurely.

The Christmas club account is an example of what is both good and bad about our society. On the plus side, we are fortunate to have the ease of payroll deductions to fund accounts throughout the year that can then be used to pay seasonal spending around the holidays. The downside is that our mentality is such that many of us look at these funds as having only one use, which is to spend every dime. No thought is ever given to permanently saving some of what has been set aside. Nevertheless, I do maintain it is at least commendable that such individuals are funding ahead of future purchases.

With pension plans no longer as common today, I have seen over the last two decades a significant shift in how large companies have extended bonus plans to more of the employee base. Before, such plans were commonly skewed toward management. However, the recent change in corporate strategy has been to reduce financial commitments far out in time, such as pensions, and instead make annual bonus payments each year, assuming profitability and operational goals are achieved. If the goals are not met, the company is off the hook for making payment, unlike the pension plans.

Many of the annual bonus plans are paid out after a December year-end when financial results have been measured, typically in February or early March. Unfortunately, this payment cycle follows on the heels of the holiday season, and it has been my observation that individuals will loosen their spending habits in anticipation of their bonus payout. If a maximum payout has been received over the last couple of years, it becomes an easy mind-set to assume the same payout will be received for the current year.

The annual bonus is the first of two things with which one shouldn't fall in love. To be sure, one should never commit to buy something with uncertain money. The world of business is way too unforgiving, as economic conditions can suddenly turn sour, or unexpected costs can come from nowhere and deflate earnings for the year. A rewind to 2008 is all that needs to be said here.

Prudent financial behavior, therefore, dictates that one simply wait until money is in hand before making the desired purchase. If the money never materializes, that is never a good thing. However, refraining from buying at least keeps the individual in a neutral financial position.

To continue the theme of love affairs, *the second thing one should avoid is the dependence upon income tax refunds.* Being a tax practitioner, I see this both in my personal practice as well as in the proliferation of advertisements on television for quick refunds. By the first of January, tax preparation and tax software companies are already out of the gate to help us prepare our tax returns as quickly as possible.

While I have no issue with getting tax returns done early, I am amazed as to the financial costs that individuals choose in getting their refunds on an immediate basis. Very simply, many Americans are making poor financing decisions because they are so strapped for cash, and this, to me, is a source of significant concern. If major finance companies are intertwined with tax preparation companies in funding the rapid refund, you know the profits to be made are huge. And if profits are that attractive, then the law of winners and losers suggests that individual taxpayers are footing the bill.

What probably concerns me even more than the ill-advised financing costs in getting the tax refunds is the pressing need for Americans to get their money as quickly as possible. It just seems there is such an unhealthy number of taxpayers who are in desperate need of instant funds.

Furthermore, unlike twenty years ago when refunds typically took four to six weeks to receive, we are living in the age when electronic filing ensures a turnaround of approximately ten days. But for so many individuals this is too long a wait, and that is what is so worrisome to me. So we choose instead to pay high embedded interest rates and fees to get refunds back perhaps a week earlier.

My personal observations

From a tax practice view, I find it to be very common that many taxpayers assume that past years' refunds will continue into the future. When I find myself in the unfortunate position of telling taxpayers they owe money to the IRS, so often I hear the words "last year we got a big refund" coming right back at me. For one, I can often hear the financial distress in their voice, as if there are large bills to pay that were incurred under the assumption of receiving the usual tax refund.

Second, I find it alarming that so many are out of touch with their tax situation, as conditions can easily change from the prior year. For instance, a couple who typically receives a refund may have had one spouse to receive unemployment benefits for a large part of the current year. Typically, such payments have taxes withheld at a very low rate, or perhaps none at all. Therefore, when tax time rolls around, the lower withholding often results in a significant payment due rather than a refund.

Also, many of the tax breaks for middle-income Americans are such that an increase in income from the previous year, though good from an earnings standpoint, may trigger the phaseout of favorable tax credits such as the child credit and college education credit. This is a very common occurrence, which makes it challenging for practitioners like me to adequately explain to clients the unfortunate change from receiving large refunds to suddenly owing tax. For many, such bad news can be very unsettling.

What I wish to convey from a discussion of these two items, bonuses and tax refunds, is that the underlying reason for financial distress isn't so much the negative news itself, whether it be a small bonus or no refund, but rather that so many individuals are spending everything they make. Being raised modestly, I understand that many families have significant financial burdens and challenges. To this end, many have no choice but to spend income as fast as it is earned.

However, I have also witnessed many individuals and couples having good to very good incomes, only to continually upgrade their spending as fast as additional income is received. Going back a bit to our perceptions of needs and wants, I could waste countless words in my attempt to suggest how people should spend their money. But we are all different, and much of my personal bias would fall on deaf ears. Nonetheless, I do feel the message is applicable to those who spend practically all they make.

Simply put, don't spend until you have the money in hand, whether it be a bonus payment, a tax refund, or both. We as optimistic and giving Americans have this tendency to succumb to mass advertising and Christmas cheer, buying goods in excess of our means, yet thinking of that potential bonus or tax refund that will be there to bail us out in late winter. The optimism is great to have, and that is part of what makes America a great place to live.

However, all it takes is one year of bad news, and we can find ourselves behind normal in meeting our obligations. As a backstop, this is all too frequently where credit card financing rears its ugly head. Look in your mailbox in January, or watch the television ads. The credit card companies come out of the woodwork each year. They want to lend money, and they want you to pay on their terms.

Christmas club accounts are not the best, but for free spenders I suggest having multiple accounts, perhaps one for the holidays, one for vacation, and another for a rainy-day fund. Saving now and spending later is so much more conducive to financial health than spending now and taking care of details later. Relying upon corporate board rooms, tax accountants, and impacts of changing tax laws is simply not worth the risk of having to be later bailed out by a credit card company.

Summary Points
- *Never assume a bonus payout until the cash is received.*
- *Never assume a tax refund until you sign the return.*
- *In both cases, never commit to large purchases ahead of receiving the funds.*

Chapter 16 Exercise

<u>As a self-analysis, answer the following questions</u>:

	YES	NO
(1) If your employer has a bonus plan, do you keep up with current company financial information rather than just assume there will be some payout?	☐	☐
(2) Do you ever make a large purchase ahead of a bonus payout?	☐	☐
(3) Do you view a tax refund as something that should be spent?	☐	☐
(4) Have you ever used a bonus or tax refund to pay down debt?	☐	☐
(5) Have you ever made a large purchase before filing your tax return, only to find out later your refund was much smaller than expected, or you were having to pay tax?	☐	☐
(6) Do you use rapid refund to get a tax refund as quickly as possible? If so, have you stopped to calculate the effective interest rate you are paying in fees?	☐	☐

    This is simply an exercise to make you stop and think about the concepts mentioned in choosing to show patience ahead of uncertain income and refunds. In an ideal world, questions one and four would be checked "yes," and the remaining answers would be "no."

Chapter 17

It Bears Repeating—Part I

So often in life I have come across people who for whatever reason cannot seem to let a topic of conversation rest. The reasons for such can be simple arrogance—thinking what is being said just has to be rehashed because the matter at hand is so important. Other times, the person doing the talking may simply forget what he or she just said, and so we get to hear the story again.

On a personal level, I have always made it a goal to try my best to never repeat the same story or to share a topic of advice with someone more than once. In fact, there have probably been times I should have spoken up but chose not to because I couldn't remember if I had shared the topic of conversation earlier.

However, here is a time that I choose to blatantly toss aside my personal preference and repeat a belief to the point of being obnoxious. Luckily, this chapter is brief and direct, but I sincerely believe the message is as important as you will find anywhere.

In chapter 15, we discussed the use of the credit card and how it can actually benefit certain users. However, in the zero-sum game of life, we know that winners are always propped up by losers. Recall the groups two and three users of credit cards.

After I had written the earlier chapter, I happened to notice a particular disclosure on one of my credit card statements that I had never before given attention. Specifically, this was something new that came from added government requirements placed upon financial institutions as a result of the 2008 financial crisis. To my point, the statement for the month was one having a balance of just over $2,000.

In this case, I paid the balance in full, keeping true to my principles. However, what caught my eye were the following:

1. *If just the minimum monthly payment was made, it would take about eleven years to pay off the balance! And this was assuming no more purchases would be made on the card during that time!*
2. *If I chose to make a $73 extra payment above the minimum, it would take around three years to pay off the balance, again assuming no more purchases in the meantime.*

The part of this disclosure that made such an impact upon me was the length of time it would take to pay off the balance without using the card in the meantime. How realistic is that assumption in our world of daily consumption of goods and services? Assuming I purchased a $2,000 couch, how smart would it be to rely upon a credit card to finance such a purchase over eleven years?

We all know that credit cards aren't meant to serve us for just one month of purchases, and then making minimum payments for over ten years. If so, we would be much better off going to the local credit union and getting a loan with a much lower interest rate.

Have you ever stopped to wonder why credit card companies ask for such a low minimum payment each month? The answer is that they have a nice deal going on, probably financed at least at 18 percent. So why would they give an incentive to pay down the balance quicker? This is their investment, so it only makes sense to extend the terms as long as possible.

I do not choose to look at credit card companies as the enemy. After all, we as consumers are the ones who feed the demand for convenience of the card by having to make only minimal payments each month. But my point in rehashing this topic is simply this. So many Americans are helplessly mired in credit card debt and simply fail to take strong steps to remove themselves from its grip. Perhaps such widespread lack of action is due to a feeling of helplessness, or being naïve to the dire straits in which many find themselves.

In simple terms, either pay off the monthly balance in full, using either your cash or financing with the lowest rate debt you can get, or cut the credit card and rely upon cash to make future purchases. The impact otherwise could end up being astronomical over time.

CHAPTER 18

It Bears Repeating—Part 2

SIMILAR TO THE LAST chapter, I have taken the liberty to lecture on a theme that I adamantly consider worthy of repeat. This time, the topic is retirement planning. Similar to the last chapter, I will be brief and to the point.

Today's employment isn't nearly the same as employment from a generation ago. Unless you work for a state or federal government, true employer-funded pensions are becoming scarcer and scarcer every year. As was mentioned earlier, employers have chosen to take future retirement obligations off their backs and put the responsibility upon the employees. On a different topic, employers in general have chosen to abandon the promise of health benefits after retirement due to the extreme cost and uncertainty.

While I do not like the trends that have taken place, I cannot say that I disagree with the changes made by the employer community. After all, we as consumers like the best quality at the lowest price, particularly here in the United States. As a result, companies are forced to squeeze costs to stay competitive. Not surprisingly, pensions and health care have been the so-called low-hanging fruit.

It does no good to fret over things beyond our control, or worse, to complain and do nothing to help the situation. Just as the credit card problem is an issue that takes away from *what we have*, the retirement problem is an issue that is failing to address planning for *what we need to have in the future*. Both scare me so much as to the future of our country.

THE POWER OF SACRIFICE

What would you do if you were asked if you wanted a 4 percent raise, with no strings attached, in addition to your normal raise? Obviously, that is a stupid question at best, and we know what your answer would be. What if your employer added a stipulation that in order to get the 4 percent raise, you also had to fork over 4 percent of your own money, sounding much like a gain of zero? Amazingly, you have just gone from elation to skepticism and probably repeated the old axiom that "nobody is going to give you anything in life."

Ironically, I have just presented a solution for many of the population in regard to how to confront the issue of proper retirement planning. Sadly, many individuals choose to free up spending money by reducing their 401(k) contributions, or perhaps by doing away with them altogether. Yet, if these same individuals would simply choose to fund their 401(k) at the level to achieve the maximum employer match, the end result, by comparison, would be amazing. As stated earlier, if need of cash is an issue, my recommendation would be to rely upon the 401(k) as a loan, thereby keeping the investment in the 401(k) and having loan payment discipline through automatic pay withdrawals.

Unfortunately, it all too often has been my observation that individuals who have chosen to either reduce or eliminate their 401(k) contributions wait far too long to restore their contributions back to the prior levels. By doing this, individuals are essentially relying upon Social Security to be their source of retirement, which in itself is no longer a guarantee.

Before I belabor this point, let's take a quick example of two thirty-year-old individuals who work for the same employer, where there is a 401(k) match, dollar for dollar up to 5 percent. Individual A chooses to fund his retirement at 5 percent of pay, thereby realizing a match of 5 percent from his employer. On the other hand, individual B wishes to live a more upscale lifestyle and sets aside only 1 percent of his pay, getting a 1 percent match.

As with so many things in life, months turn to years, and years to decades, and so often with these types of financial decisions nothing changes once a decision is put in place. At an assumed average salary of $60,000 and a rate of return of 8 percent over thirty-five years, here is what the 401(k) balances would be at retirement age of 65 for each individual:

Individual A, $1,147,000
Individual B, $229,000

In the first case, individual A will have $210,000 of his own money invested, while individual B will have $42,000 personally invested. In both cases, over 18 percent of their own money will make up the retirement balances. However, the real difference lies in the dollars of matching contributions from the employer and related earnings for individual A. Effectively, he sold himself on the strange logic of giving up 4 percent of his current pay to get a 4 percent raise in dollars he couldn't touch until retirement.

At age sixty-five, the true raise that A earned for himself by choosing the 5 percent withholding versus 1 percent equals the difference of $918,000 between the balances of A and B at retirement. Spread over thirty-five years of employment, this comes to an average of $26,000 per year above that accumulated at retirement by individual B.

Compared to his average annual pay of $60,000, this is the same as a 43 percent raise in future dollars for A, all achieved by signing up on day one for the 5 percent match rather than the 1 percent. In very simple terms, A chose to put an extra 4 percent of his own money to work, and in doing so took an extra 4 percent with him in the form of free money from his employer. Collectively, this extra 8 percent amazingly yielded an additional $918,000 at retirement.

Never choose a 401(k) election that gives anything less than the maximum company match. Do what you must to make it work, whether it is refinancing or consolidating debts, cutting back on personal lifestyle, selling luxuries you don't truly need, or some combination of these. To do otherwise is the same as taking a suitcase full of cash and flushing it down the toilet.

CHAPTER 19

Texting behind Home Plate

BEING AN ACCOUNTANT IS somewhat equivalent to being issued a license to not have fun in life, or so it sounds coming from the common stereotype of many people. Granted, I'm not the daredevil type who jumps off cliffs, nor do I have any desire to scale Mount Everest anytime soon. However, at the risk of destroying the myth, I do love sports. Give me a basketball, baseball, or football game, and I'm in just as much as the next person. So for the record, accountants do have fun every now and then.

Along similar lines, I will confess to not being "hip" to the current generation of high-tech communications. I have a few strong reasons for being who I am; among those are the facts that I have neither the intellectual knack for picking up on the intricacies of computer technology, nor do I have the desire. Also, I'm somewhat of an old-school person who still adheres to the values of personal communication and the meaning of a handshake.

To the day I die, I know for certain that I will always keep this feeling that texting, in particular, has done very little to advance the cause for mankind. For certain situations in business and every now and then for personal use, I realize it has its place. But overall, I think the downsides will forever outweigh the positives. Attention spans have shrunk, no one knows how to relax, and, most of all, driving safety has become just downright scary.

As I have asked my son and daughter many times, why can't people just call and talk? It's almost as if we have chosen to take the more difficult way and express our thoughts one letter at a time. I just don't get it, but enough of preaching reserved for my children.

All of this profoundness does have a point I would like to make that pertains to financial behavior. Several times I have had the great opportunity to watch the St. Louis Cardinals in person, every now and then while occupying a very good seat behind the dugout. To me, that is a thrill that every sports fan should get to enjoy. However, I do have one observation I wish to share that I've noticed from watching on television and in person.

Have you ever observed fans behind home plate during a game? These folks sit in what I consider marquee seats that allow one to practically have the ball game in the equivalent of one's living room. What has amazed me is how often I notice so many of these fans with their cell phones, texting during the middle of the game. This began to catch my attention about five years ago when texting became quite popular.

On the one hand, I'm fully on board with one being enthusiastic and wishing to either share a photo with a friend, or calling to talk about the game. However, at the other extreme I am amazed how one can be sitting so close to the best athletes in the world in the midst of competition, yet take the time to look away and text! And I'm not talking about once or twice during the game. This is seemingly all through the game. Is there anything in this world that can trump texting?

COMPLACENCY VERSUS CONTENTMENT

The thoughts from baseball and texting take me back to a Sunday school class back in 1987 taught by a fellow named David Crockett. For whatever reason, I have always remembered what David talked about that Sunday morning, which was the topic of *complacency* versus *contentment*. Being the tender age of twenty-two at that time, I didn't quite appreciate the lesson like I do now a quarter century later.

Quite simply, both are issues that keep so many people from realizing true potential and reaching genuine happiness. On one side, complacency keeps us from pushing the envelope and challenging ourselves to see what we can achieve. Perhaps because of fear of failure or lack of support from family, many people are not willing to take chances in an effort to better themselves. A common slogan is "give 'em eight, and hit the gate," suggesting that people feel they owe forty hours a week to their employers and nothing more.

In my opinion, one who complains about his or her financial status in life and is complacent often has no right to be complaining, especially in a free country such as ours. Granted, there are different obstacles for us all, but nothing will stand against us more than a complacent attitude. If an employer is willing to reward those who go above and beyond the norm, then one wishing to advance must get rid of the minimum-effort mentality.

To me, complacency has this inherent and infectious trait that over time will challenge such qualities as neatness, being prompt, attention to detail, and even self-respect. In my opinion, we all should do a self-evaluation every now and then to assess our level of motivation in overcoming complacency. Otherwise, we face the risk of not achieving our true potential in life.

On the other side of the issue is contentment, which I feel is the more dangerous of the two qualities, especially in regard to finances and lifestyle. Going back to complacency, this generally suggests one who is getting by in life, perhaps not making the salary he or she could, but at the same time taking that salary and being able to meet his or her family's needs and wants in a comfortable manner. In short, one who is complacent is generally content.

However, the issue on the contentment side isn't so much about those who are complacent as it is those who are not complacent. In other words, the apparent higher achievers are those who have to periodically question whether they are content with their lives, especially financially. No doubt, this can be a tough struggle for many as the goals of "I want to do better" and "I want to be content" must be reconciled. In my opinion, this type of person is the most vulnerable to being miserable, unlike the individual who chooses

Fields of Green

complacency. It seems ironic, but I truly believe this is the case for many.

Looking over one's shoulder

Going back to one texting behind home plate, when is enough really "enough"? How much do we have to keep absorbing in the way of leisure and entertainment to truly satisfy our wants and keep our attention? To me, this is at the core of the two things I mentioned earlier that are having such a negative impact on household net worth—the credit card and excessive spending, particularly on automobiles. If our neighbor has something, then it seems we must have it also, and right now. If a coworker is going to an exotic place for vacation, we must go somewhere equally as nice.

In short, the credit card and reckless spending are merely symptoms of the real problem of not being content in life. Even the high achievers on Wall Street who make hundreds of thousands of dollars fall prey to the rat race. If you don't believe it, just wait for the news articles that will appear in the early part of the year detailing the anxiety of investment bankers awaiting the outcomes of their bonuses. And then we wonder why excess and greed exist on Wall Street, not to mention the inherent cheating that takes place to make the game work.

Personally, I have no desire to ever put myself in that position of living capitalism to its utmost. Instead, I hope I will always choose the path of working hard, treating all people equally, and hoping for a little good luck to guide me along toward a happy retirement. Without getting on a soap box, it just seems that Wall Street mentalities have crept to Main Street over the past several years, making the state of contentment that much more of a challenge for us all.

On a personal level, I can only look back to experiences I've had growing up and more recently that at least confirm to me my feelings of contentment. During my senior year of high school, I was on a basketball team that didn't have a starter over five feet ten. Despite losing our first seven games, we nonetheless hung together and discovered ways to win, beating teams we had no business beating.

Even though our eventual record of 10–15 was unimpressive to the average person, I look back at that year knowing there's not a thing I would go back and change if I could, because we truly did the best we could with the abilities we had. And for that reason, that year will always be one of the best of my life.

On an even more personal level, I decided to usher in my decade of turning forty by running a marathon in Huntsville, Alabama, in December 2004. Never one to run track in school, I surprised myself by training over one thousand miles over the six months leading up to the race. Despite finishing an hour and twenty minutes behind the winner, you have no idea how thrilled I was to finish that race without ever stopping to walk!

Not once did I ever single out someone I wanted to pass during the race, but rather it was all about me against my weakness to start walking, or even quit. It became a test of wills that I won, and for that achievement I will always be proud. And looking back, I still have such a feeling of contentment that I really did the best I could, irrespective of what others around me did.

And finally, from a financial perspective, I perhaps could have done better from a career standpoint by choosing to take a job in Nashville after graduation from college. After all, the exposures to big clients and huge opportunities often are found where the skyscrapers exist. But instead, I chose to stay close to my hometown and keep in touch with friends and family. That was my source of contentment, rather than trying to keep up with the Joneses. To this day, I have never regretted that decision or wondered how much more money I could have earned.

So much is easier said than done, but I wholeheartedly believe that contentment is at the core of achieving good financial health. To borrow a time-tested phrase, one should always look ahead to the task when plowing, because looking back will cause one to veer off the straight path. Similarly, looking over one's shoulder in today's world to see where others are will only cause one to become distracted, and then perhaps discontented.

In short, my advice to anyone is to do the best you can, where you can, and when you can. If so, all else that truly matters should take care of itself.

CHAPTER 20

I Think I'm Done

As I attempt to close my thoughts, I have this feeling of uncertainty as to the value of my efforts put forward in this book. To put it mildly, this has been a challenge far beyond what I had imagined. My goal was simplicity, yet that tends to go out the window when factoring in the various human elements.

I look back and try to think of something I should have added, and to be honest, nothing comes to mind. Perhaps this is acknowledgment of my fragile limitations. Nonetheless, I firmly believe that addition of more facts and opinions can at some point translate into subtraction of meaningful content. Therefore, I hold fast to my opinion that no more needs to be said in the way of financial advice.

On a personal note, farming gave me so many opportunities to confront challenges logically, many times in the face of uncertain weather. But I think the most important thing I learned was that you do the best you can under the circumstances, whether it is preparing the soil, choosing the right seed, or scheduling the time to sell. I learned especially to appreciate the fact that Mother Nature always had the final say in the matter, despite the best plans and actions. Without a doubt, we all are at the mercy of things beyond our control. If we only acknowledge that fact, our humility will serve us well.

Unfortunately, humility has no real place on Wall Street, in particular. Being a firm believer in the free market system, I nonetheless am a skeptic of the arrogance and greed that is seemingly inherent in our great economy. CEOs in many companies are where they are due to backstabbing and office politics, rather than from years of serving others in the company. Sadly, many of these individuals fail to add any value to the shareholders of the company. If you don't believe that, then you haven't been reading the stories in the newspapers about corruption in the business world.

Personally, I have a very good accounting job today for two reasons. For one, very capable men and women in our production facility manufacture a great aluminum product. Second, consumers of automobiles and residential housing products create the demand in the pipeline. With no demand for aluminum, there would be no billet produced, and consequently no job for me. I am merely a support person for the great workers in our company.

Along similar lines, a CEO of a large health products company has a job because of good workers making its products. Furthermore, the CEO ultimately owes his good fortune to the fact that elderly people get sick, people get injured, and babies get diaper rashes. Pure and simple, it all goes back to needs and wants in society. You will hardly hear those thoughts from a CEO because most are more focused on their perceived prestige in society rather than on genuine service to their employees and shareholders.

On a simpler note, the green you see in the field is the real reason we all exist. Going back to Mr. Maslow, if you take away our food, all other things really don't matter. Our gym memberships, phone gadgets, sports cars, and other such extras would be worth nothing to us without food to eat.

And before you suggest my thoughts seem strange, stop and think about people in Ethiopia and other such countries. Those folks don't care a thing about being overlooked in the toy lines. Rather, they would just like to have a little food to give their children.

Corn crops don't fall out of the sky and suddenly occupy grain bins every fall. Rather, they and other grains come about from the hard work and dedication of some of the smartest people on earth, not to mention a lot of help from above. To put it bluntly, city folk are where they are because of country folk. Remember that the next time you drive down the country road and observe acres and acres of ripening green crops. Those don't just appear on the landscape by accident.

If you think I may sound a little biased toward the country, I will give you that without dispute. However, what I wish to establish in the way of credibility is that I have experienced both extremes of living the farm life and living in the corporate world. What I have observed on a consistent basis is that nothing is as complicated in the corporate world as people want you to believe. But for many, that is their veil of insecurity. Along the same thought, nothing in the farm life is as simple as farmers let on, but that is only a reflection that comes from the inherent humility of most farmers.

As an example, I have witnessed firsthand in the corporate world those who would intentionally delay getting their work done in order to finish right at the deadline, thus giving the appearance of doing something grand, which actually was quite simple. I like to call that playing politics. On the farm, that's called being lazy. Yes, there is a reason why farmers are the most efficient operators in the world. I've been there and done that, and I've been there and done the other. I know the difference.

Throughout the book, I have attempted to the best of my ability to present a framework of observations and advice that break down what we often consider intimidating and complex into something simple to understand. That has truly been my overarching theme. It seems that today's media tries to glorify legal and financial matters into something that borders on rocket science, yet most of the true complexities lie in the fine print that must be written because we as a society are so afraid of lawsuits.

In short, my point is that folks on Wall Street have nothing on those on Main Street when it comes to talent and smarts. Rather, it mostly boils down to where we want to work and live, with whom we want to be seen, and how we want to spend our leisure time. Our focus, whether Wall Street or Main Street, should be on a gradual accumulation of net worth, not how much we earn and how much we spend on things that glitter. Wearing wingtips Monday through Friday as an adult never did any more for me than wearing steel-toe boots when I was a kid on the farm.

The fields of green will forever be my source of inspiration, heritage, and hope. Simplicity is strength, and no matter how complicated you may think your life is, whether financially or otherwise, every problem can be broken down to its simplest form. The problem with credit card debt may be discipline. The problem with excess spending may be ego. The problem with savings may be selfishness.

Just like the corn seed, we all have certain qualities within us, both good and bad. We really can't control who we are, but we can affect what we become by practicing discipline and common sense. This is the equivalent of keeping the weeds out of a crop in anticipation of future rains. We don't know when the rains will come, yet we want to be fully prepared to maximize results when opportunity comes our way.

It is my sincere wish that somehow, in some way, you discover how to simplify your life financially. Take the time to slow down, enjoy more of what you have now, and set aside all savings that you can for an even better life when you retire. To me, that is the true definition of wealth.

Nothing worthwhile is easy, nor should it ever be. To that end, I firmly believe that financial rewards will inevitably come later from the sacrifices and smart decisions that you make today.

Thank you for being my audience.

www.ingramcontent.com/pod-product-compliance
Lightning Source LLC
Chambersburg PA
CBHW030751180526
45163CB00003B/977